Poem into Poem

Reading and writing poems with students of English

Alan Maley and Sandra Moulding

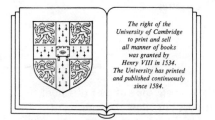

The right of the
University of Cambridge
to print and sell
all manner of books
was granted by
Henry VIII in 1534.
The University has printed
and published continuously
since 1584.

Cambridge University Press
Cambridge
London   New York   New Rochelle
Melbourne   Sydney

To
Alan Duff
poet and friend

Published by the Press Syndicate of the University of Cambridge
The Pitt Building, Trumpington Street, Cambridge CB2 1RP
32 East 57th Street, New York, NY 10022, USA
10 Stamford Road, Oakleigh, Melbourne 3166, Australia

© Cambridge University Press 1985

First published 1985

Printed in Great Britain at The Pitman Press, Bath

ISBN 0 521 31856 4 Book
ISBN 0 521 30005 3 Set of 2 cassettes

PP

Contents

Thanks

We are especially grateful to our friends Andrew Wright, Mike Swan, Pat Early and Alan Duff for generously allowing us to use their writings in this book.

We would also like to thank Alison Baxter and Alison Silver for their patient and painstaking editorial work, which transformed a heap of typescript into a book.

To the student

This book will introduce you to some memorable poems in English and help you to understand them better. It will also suggest ways in which you can produce poems of your own.

Perhaps this kind of book raises some questions in your mind:

Why use poetry to learn English?

— The first answer is, 'why not?' Poetry is a special type of English, just as scientific or newspaper English are also special – in different ways. It deserves study as much as they do, perhaps more, since poetry is the type of English which touches our personal feelings most closely. And personal feelings are as important in a foreign language as they are in our own language.
— Poetry can also help us to assimilate the typical rhythms of a language. (That is why the poems in this book have been recorded.)
— What is more, poems are often very easy to remember. They stick in our minds without conscious effort. One reason for this is that they frequently repeat patterns of sound or words.
— The topics which poems talk about are in themselves interesting – and important. When we are learning a foreign language as an adult we need to have significant things to think and talk about. Poems offer this. They give us something worthwhile to discuss.

All right, but why should we write, as well as read, poems?

— The process of composing poems, especially if it is done in groups, leads to *real* discussion, about something that matters to you.
— It also allows you to try out different ways of saying the same thing. And to make different combinations of words and sentences. This process of 'playing' with language is important in developing your confidence in using it.
— It gives you a purpose in writing, and allows you to bring in your personal feelings and ideas. Many other types of writing in a foreign language do not encourage this.

1

To the student

But won't it be too difficult for me?

The objective of this book is to make it as easy for you as possible. This is done in the following ways:
- Before you even start to read the poems, there are activities which help you 'tune in' to or become familiar with the topic of the unit.
- Any 'difficult' vocabulary in the poems is either explained or given special attention. You are also encouraged to use a dictionary wherever necessary.
- The aim of the activities is to help you understand the overall meaning of the poems. You do not need to be a literature specialist.
- Much of the language you will need for writing the poems comes from recorded conversations or from earlier activities in the unit. You are not asked to make superhuman creative efforts.
- In most of the activities, you will be sharing information, opinions and ideas with a partner or in a group. In other words, you are not left alone with your problems.

So what does a 'unit' look like?

- First there is a section called *Warming up*. It prepares you for the theme of the poems which follow. You may be asked to do activities in connection with a picture, make notes on a recorded conversation, or perhaps read a brief prose passage. These activities all involve discussion with a partner or in groups.
- You will then listen to the first *Poem* as you read it. This is followed by activities aimed at helping you to understand it.
- The same procedure follows for the second *Poem* (and in Unit 1 for the third and fourth *Poems*).
- A section on *Writing* usually follows. This contains activities leading you to produce your own poems, usually in groups. This also involves discussion of your own and other groups' work.
- Finally there is a poem for you to read and listen to on your own, with no work attached – simply for your enjoyment.

▶ Means that the poem, prose extract or conversation is recorded on the cassette. (For copyright reasons not all the extracts are recorded.)

⌐O Means that you will find the answers in the key at the back of the book.

2

Enjoyment is the keynote of the book. We hope you will enjoy using it as much as we enjoyed writing it.

▶ ## *The Language Tree*

Out of the language tree
The leaves float down.
Whirling, they criss and cross,
Writing new patterns on the ground,
Slowly coding this year's messages.

Below, the wadded strata
From past years
Distil and mature old meanings.

And down among the roots,
Half-forgotten, skeletal memories
Muted by the loam,
Stir in their sleep,
Mutter and moan.

And way above, twig ends,
Bud within bud, dream
Of meanings for next year,
And the next, and the next.

Every year the same tree,
Roughly the same shape and size.
And every year a subtle
Change of size and shape;
A small surprise –
A limited escape.

(Alan Maley)

1 Who is today?

'Days are where we live.' So it is very natural that people associate different days with different things.

Warming up

▶ 🔑 1. Listen to the recording. You will hear a man and a woman talking about the colours they associate with the days of the week. Write the colours in the grid under *Man* or *Woman*.

	Man	Why	Woman	Why
Monday				
Tuesday				
Wednesday				
Thursday				
Friday				
Saturday				
Sunday				

2. Now discuss your completed grid with a partner. Do you both have the same answers?

▶ ▅▅◦ 3. Now listen to the recording again. This time make brief notes in the grid on why the speakers have chosen these colours. Fill in *Why* in the grid.

4. Now write down the colour which *you* associate with each day, e.g. Monday – black
    Tuesday – blue, etc.
Then compare your notes with your partner.

5. In groups of four try to make a poem which uses the association of each day. Each of you should first of all work on your own, writing out a sentence about the associations of each day, using the pattern '... day is ...' (e.g. Monday is bad moods). Then compare your ideas as a group. Choose the best sentence for each day, and combine them into a poem.

Here is an example:

▶
>Sunday is warm sheets
>Monday is drab streets
>Tuesday is all grey
>Wednesday is a tasteless day
>Thursday is thin lips
>Friday is fish and chips
>Saturday is sports, TV and friends –
>A pity that it ever ends!

When you have finished, compare your poem with one written by another group.

Reading: Poems 1 and 2

1. Read this traditional rhyme about Solomon Grundy as you listen to the recording.

▶ ## A Traditional Rhyme

>Solomon Grundy,
>Born on Monday,
>Christened on Tuesday,
>Married on Wednesday,
>Took ill on Thursday,
>Worse on Friday,
>Died on Saturday,
>Buried on Sunday –
>And that was the end
>Of Solomon Grundy.

2. Now compare it with this poem.

▶ ## Solomon Grundy

>Solomon Grundy,
>Bored on Tuesday,
>Manic on Wednesday,
>Panic on Thursday,
>Drunk on Friday,
>Hung over on Saturday,
>Slept on Sunday,

Back to work on Monday –
That's the life
For Solomon Grundy.

(Martin Bell)

Writing

When somebody copies the form of someone else's poem, often with a humorous intention, we call it a parody.

In pairs try to write your own simple parody of Solomon Grundy. Here is another example:

►   Solomon Grundy,
     Happy on Sunday,
     Sad on Monday,
     Tired on Tuesday,
     Worried on Wednesday,
     Harrassed on Thursday,
     Exhausted on Friday,
     In bed on Saturday –
     What a life
     For Solomon Grundy!

When you have finished, compare your parody with one written by another pair.

Reading: Poem 3

1.   Read the following traditional rhyme as you listen to the recording. It describes the characteristics of people born on different days of the week.

►   *A Traditional Rhyme*

     Monday's Child is full of grace.
     Tuesday's Child is fair of face.
     Wednesday's Child is loving and giving.
     Thursday's Child works hard for a living.
     Friday's Child is full of woe.
     Saturday's Child has far to go.
     And the Child that's born on the Sabbath day,
     Is bonny and blithe and good and gay.

2.   Discuss the rhyme with a partner. Do you agree with the descriptions? Which day of the week were you born on? Does the description fit you? Do you have a rhyme or saying in your language which is similar to this one?

Writing

Work in groups of seven. Each person in a group is given one day of the week. You then write a sentence to describe the characteristics of people born on that day. For example:

Monday's Child is very bright.

When everyone has written a sentence, the group puts them together to form a poem. At this stage you may decide to change a few words to make it rhyme – but this is not essential. You may also find it easier if everyone is writing a sentence with the same structure. For example:

Monday's Child likes ...

or Monday's Child is good at ...

or Monday's Child has ..., etc.

When you have finished, compare your poem with another group.

Reading: Poem 4

1.   The poem *Days* treats each day of the week as if it were a person. First of all read it through, day by day, and check with a partner that you understand all the expressions the writer uses.

► *Days*

MONDAY
You'd better not try anything
just don't try anything
that's all.
You're all the same
you days.
Give you an inch ...
Well
I've got my eye on you
and I'm feeling light

fast
and full of aggro
so just watch it
OK?

TUESDAY
Listen, Tuesday
I'm sorry
I wasn't very nice to you.
It was *sweet* of you
to give me all those stars
when you said goodbye.
They must have cost a fortune
and they really were
just
what I've always wanted.

WEDNESDAY
Cracks, spills, burns, bills, broken cups, stains, wrong numbers,
     missed trains:
you're doing it on purpose
aren't you?
Trying it on
to see how far you can go.
I swear to you
if the phone rings again
while I'm in the bath
I'll pull it out
and ram it down your throat.

THURSDAY
'A difficult day for Aries
caution is advisable
in business dealings
setbacks possible
in affairs of the heart.'
Thursday, my friend
if we've got to get
through all these hours together
we might as well do it
with as little trouble
as possible.
You keep to your side of the horoscope
and I'll keep to mine.

⋙→

FRIDAY
Day like a shroud
ten feet down
black
in an airless coffin
you wrap me
in my own
clinging
loathsome
sticky skin.
I scream
and you laugh.

SATURDAY
Day
oh day
I love your perfume
(you put on daffodils
just for me)
and your yellow eye
sparkling
and the sexy way
you rub up
against me
day
I love you.

SUNDAY
Sunday and I
got drunk together
and you know
it turns out
we went to the same school.
He's a bit strange
at first
but actually
he's not a bad chap
when you get to know him
old Sunday.

(Michael Swan)

2. Discuss each day with your partner. Do you agree with the way they are described?

Writing

In pairs, use the following framework to write a similar poem.
(Wherever there are dots ... it means you should complete the line in
your own way.)

> *MONDAY*
> What an old rascal you are!
>
> Don't think you ... *can always bring a bad day,*
>
> I'm watching ... *to try and catch you out,*
>
> So just ... *be careful what you say!*
>
> *TUESDAY*
> Well, I suppose I'll have to ...
> Tuesday, you're really not ...
> How do you expect me to ...?
> Sorry if I've offended you, but ...
>
> *WEDNESDAY*
> You're getting on my ...
> How do you think I can possibly ...?
> If you are ..., I'll ...
> Just because ..., you needn't
> Think you can ...
>
> *THURSDAY*
> Who knows what ... today?
> Thursday, you have no special ...
> I just can't get excited ...
> Why don't you try to ...?
>
> *FRIDAY*
> You are so ...
> I can't stand the way you ...
> You fill me with ...
> I just can't wait ...
>
> *SATURDAY*
> This is what I've been ...
> You smell ...
> You taste ...
> You sound ...
> You feel ...
> How can I ever ...?

⋙→

SUNDAY
Sunday and I went . . .
And do you know what happened?
Well . . .
So I said to old Sunday,
' . . .'
And he said, ' . . .'
Sometimes life feels really . . .

When you have finished, compare your poem with another pair.

Reading alone

These poems are to read on your own.

► ## *A Day in the Life of . . .*

'It was a Sunday I met your father.
Midsummer it was, in the park.
I still remember his waistcoat
And the proud way he held his head.
I still can't think he's dead.

The Saturday we got married
It snowed all day. Freezing it was.
A white wedding
But a warm bedding.
Difficult to believe for you I know.
But we didn't always show
The things we felt.
It doesn't mean – oh never mind.
There isn't time.

You were born on a,
Let me see, a Monday.
Midnight it was. What a business!
You the first, and in a thunderstorm too.

Not like your sister –
A Tuesday in July,
Midday it was . . .

Sorry. It's too late to cry.
Funny the way you die.'
Friday at eight
It was.

(Alan Maley)

▶ ## *Sunday, bloody Sunday*

sun scrubbed
sky scoured
wind rinsed
earth showered
clouds brushed
horizon pressed
air washed
Sunday dressed

ponds permed
fountains waved
shrubs trimmed
lawns shaved
statues primmed
flowers perfumed
paths combed
park groomed

socks shed
ankles bared
noses covered
nails pared
pages flipped
smoke blown
stitches slipped
snaps shown

balls kicked
sticks thrown
ropes skipped
kites flown

⟫→

Who is today?

bottles sucked
straws sipped
ices licked
cups lipped

sky high
spirits low
life quick
Sunday slow

(Alan Duff)

2 Memories

Children talk a lot, but adults do not always listen to what they say. Yet when they do trouble to listen, they often hear some startlingly vivid uses of language. The child's mind lives in a timeless present, uncluttered by experience. Perhaps that is why we remember best the things which happened early in our lives.

Warming up

▶

Adam	have you a long pole?
Daddy	no sorry
Adam	or a ladder?
Daddy	what do you want it for?
Adam	I want to knock down the sun and break it in two and give mummy it to cook and we'll eat it
Daddy	but what will we do without the sun in the sky?
Adam	I don't like it
Daddy	what's wrong with it?
Adam	it's *boring*
Daddy	But the *sun*. I'm fond of the sun
Adam	I'll get another
Daddy	how?
Adam	I'll buy one
Daddy	where?
Adam	in Woolworths
Daddy	I'm glad I haven't got a ladder to reach the sun if that's what you would do with it
Adam	O *daddy*. (*pause*) haven't you got one I could stand on tiptoe on top of, and poke it out with a stick?

(R. D. Laing, *Conversations with Children*)

1. Try to remember some of the earliest things that happened to you as a child. Think of two incidents which particularly impressed you. Then try to draw a simple picture of each one as in the example below. (If you can remember them, write in the day, the time of year and the year it happened.)

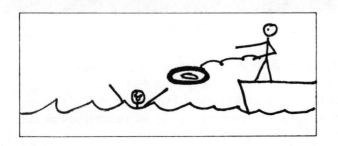

2.   Then work with a partner. Try to interpret the incidents in his or her drawings. You can ask questions too.

▶ ⚷ 3.   Listen to the recording. You will hear some people telling each other about incidents from their childhood. Make notes in the grid below. Remember, you can listen to the cassette more than once. Then compare your notes in groups of three. If you disagree, listen to the recording again.

The person	Age at the time of the event	The event	Feelings about the event
Woman 1			
Man			
Woman 2			

Reading: Poem 1

1. Read the poem *Growing Pain* as you listen to the recording.

▶ *Growing Pain*

The boy was barely five years old.
We sent him to the little school
And left him there to learn the names
Of flowers in jam jars on the sill
And learn to do as he was told.
He seemed quite happy there until
Three weeks afterwards, at night,
The darkness whimpered in his room.
I went upstairs, switched on his light,
And found him wide awake, distraught,
Sheets mangled and his eiderdown
Untidy carpet on the floor.
I said 'Why can't you sleep? A pain?'
He snuffled, gave a little moan,
And then he spoke a single word:
'Jessica.' The sound was blurred.
'Jessica? What do you mean?'
'A girl at school called Jessica,
She hurts –' he touched himself between
The heart and stomach '– she has been
Aching here and I can see her.'
Nothing I had read or heard
Instructed me in what to do.
I covered him and stroked his head.
'The pain will go, in time.' I said.

(Vernon Scannell)

Some of the words and phrases may need explanation:

whimpered: cried, in a frightened way like an animal
distraught: upset
mangled: twisted
eiderdown: a thick cover for a bed
snuffled: made sniffing sounds
blurred: not clear

2. Check your understanding of the poem with a partner. What does it tell us about:
– the boy's school, and what he did there?
– the attitude of his parents towards his education?
– the boy's feelings?
– the father's reaction?

3. There are some unusual combinations of words ('the darkness whimpered') and unusual word use ('she hurts ...', 'she has been aching here ...').

With a partner try to write out what the poet meant in everyday English. Then compare what you have written with another pair.

🔑 4. Read the poem quietly to yourself. Which lines rhyme? Use the letters a, b, c, etc. to describe the pattern. The first six lines have been done for you. Is it a regular pattern? Compare notes with your partner.

Growing Pain

The boy was barely five years old.	a
We sent him to the little school	b
And left him there to learn the names	c
Of flowers in jam jars on the sill	d
And learn to do as he was told.	a
He seemed quite happy there until	d

5. Read these quotations of things children said. Work in groups of four and try to re-write what they said in a more ordinary way.

Quotations:

a)
Adam	when do we go back to school
Jutta	the day after tomorrow
Adam	when is that?
Natasha	two sleeps

b)
	the wind is moving the clouds and shaking the branches
Natasha	is the moon shaking?

c)
	we are lying on our backs surveying the stars
Daddy	how did all this come about?
Adam	do you mean 'who made it?'?
Daddy	well not exactly, but alright
Adam	a dead man

⟫→

	Daddy	a dead man?! how do you mean?
	Adam	yes. A dead human being
d)	Adam	have you been to the *core* of the earth?
	Daddy	no
	Adam	why not? No one's been there. It's very hot and very deep
	Natasha	deeper than this table

(R. D. Laing, *Conversations with Children*)

6.   Now choose one of the quotations and use it as a part of your poem. Here is an example:

▶
    'How long before we leave?'
    'Two sleeps,' I said,
    Far away in the land of children.
    But now that I must leave you
    The day after tomorrow,
    (Using the adult speech)
    It's no longer two sleeps
    I'll have
    But two sleepless, endless nights.

Reading: Poem 2

1.   Read the poem *A Child Half-Asleep* as you listen to the recording.

▶
A Child Half-Asleep

Stealthily parting the small-hours silence,
a hardly-embodied figment of his brain
comes down to sit with me
as I work late.
Flat-footed, as though his legs and feet
were still asleep.

He sits on a stool,
staring into the fire,
his dummy dangling.

Fire ignites the small coals of his eyes.
It stares back through the holes
into his head, into the darkness.

I ask what woke him?

'A wolf dreamed me' he says.

(Tony Connor)

Some of the words and expressions may need explanation:

the small hours: the early hours of the morning (the middle of the
  night)
hardly-embodied: almost as if separated from his body
figment: something imagined
dummy: a rubber teat which young children suck to comfort themselves
a wolf: a fierce wild animal (like a wild dog)

🔑 2.   Here is what the child in the poem might have said many
years later, when describing the event. Fill in the gaps using the list of
words at the end:

My .... says that when I was very young, I came
.... in the early .... of the morning. I was
obviously   still   ....   Anyway,   I   sat   down   in
.... the fire, my .... in my mouth, and just
.... into the .... My father had been up
late .... He asked .... had woken me up.
And my ...., which he remembers to this day was, 'A
wolf .... me.'

*working, father, stared, reply, half-asleep, dreamed, downstairs,
what, hours, dummy, front of, fire*

3.   What do you think the boy meant by 'A wolf dreamed me'?
How would you normally use the verb 'dream'?
A famous Chinese philosopher, Chuanzu, told the following
story:

'I woke up from a deep sleep where I had dreamed I was a yellow butterfly. And as I woke I was not sure whether I had dreamed the butterfly or whether the butterfly had dreamed Chuanzu.'

Does this help you to understand what the child said in the poem?

4.   What similarities and differences are there between the two poems? Make a list with a partner.
Which poem did you prefer? Can you explain your reasons to your partner?

Writing

1.   Work in groups of six. Each of you should write down memories of your first school: the colours, the sounds, the tastes, the smells and the feelings.
The group should then compare notes.
2.   Still in the same group, each of you takes one area of memory (sight, sound, taste, smell, touch and feeling). Write one sentence recording your own memory of that area. Each sentence should begin with 'I remember ...'. For example:
   I remember the brown colour of the walls.
When everyone has finished, the group should combine the sentences into a single poem.
3.   Look back at the pictures you drew in *Warming up*. Write down all the words you associate with that event. Then exchange your picture and your list of words with a partner. Now you should use each other's pictures and lists to write a short poem about the incident. Compare poems when you have finished.

Reading alone

Here is a poem to read on your own.

▶   *It was Long Ago*

> I'll tell you, shall I, something I remember?
> Something that still means a great deal to me.
> It was long ago.

A dusty road in summer I remember,
A mountain, and an old house, and a tree
That stood, you know,

Behind the house. An old woman I remember
In a red shawl with a grey cat on her knee
Humming under a tree.

She seemed the oldest thing I can remember,
But then perhaps I was not more than three.
It was long ago.

I dragged on the dusty road, and I remember
How the old woman looked over the fence at me
And seemed to know

How it felt to be three, and called out, I remember
'Do you like bilberries and cream for tea?'
I went under the tree

And while she hummed, and the cat purred, I remember
How she filled a saucer with berries and cream for me
So long ago,

Such berries and such cream as I remember
I never had seen before and never see
Today, you know.

And that is almost all I can remember,
The house, the mountain, the grey cat on her knee,
Her red shawl, and the tree.

And the taste of the berries, the feel of the sun I remember,
And the smell of everything that used to be
So long ago,

Till the heat on the road outside again I remember,
And how the long dusty road seemed to have for me
No end, you know.

That is the farthest thing I can remember.
It won't mean much to you. It does to me.
Then I grew up, you see.

(Eleanor Farjeon)

3 Running away

As children grow up, there comes a point when they find themselves in conflict with their parents about a whole series of things. Sometimes, it seems to them that the only solution is to leave home.

Warming up

1. Write down on a sheet of paper the conflicts which you can remember having with your parents. Then compare notes with a partner.

Then, in groups of four, write out a list of all your points.

▶ 🔊 2. Listen to the recording. You will hear brief answers which some other people gave to the question, 'What did you and your parents disagree about?' Make notes on each reply and then compare your notes with a partner. Remember, you can listen to the cassette more than once.

Person	What did you and your parents disagree about?
Woman 1	
Man 1	
Woman 2	
Man 2	

In the same groups of four, compare your own list (from 1) with the answers on the recording.

3. In pairs, write out the questions which parents might ask themselves after their son or daughter has run away.

What ...?   Should I have ...?
Did I ...?   Perhaps I shouldn't have ...?
Was I too ...?   Why didn't I ...?

4. Read the following extract.

►   She swung her gaze round to me. She'd longed for me to be like her. 'You don't have to be that way, Margaret.'

'No, but what's the choice? To live like this, here, or to live like Alec's wife, blooming with health and children ... and as empty as a tin can.'

'Oh, Margaret.' She was shaken. 'Nora's a fine mother. They couldn't have a better mother.'

'But *I* don't want to be a mother.'

'Love ... it's not like you ...' She struggled to find her words.

'It's *just* like me! Why have I stayed like this, like I am? Being a mother – it's just the end of everything. Just to go on like that ... like any dog or cat. It makes *nothing* of me.'

She was afraid of her own anger. Her hands lay flat on the arms of the chair and she didn't look at me. It was too much. 'You're a woman, Margaret,' she said. 'What d'you reckon you're talking about?'

'Of course I'm a woman. I'm a woman, not a mother.'

'Don't you feel ... Don't you *ever* want to have children?'

'Yes. But I'm not so silly as to think that means I *have* to have them. Children ... they just ruin a woman. She becomes just a mother. Just *look* at a mother when her family have grown up and left her – groping about, wondering why she isn't a person any more, how she can fill in the day with nothing to do. Oh, Mum! I'm not trying to hurt you. But being a mother, to me, it all seems so hopeless and useless.'

'Nay, I want to hear what you think,' she said, labouring rigid in the chair. 'I'd like to know.'

'I've said. I don't want to say any more.'

(David Storey, *Flight into Camden*)

Reading: Poems 1 and 2

1. Read these two poems on your own. Then go through them with a partner, checking any unfamiliar words together.

► ## *What Has Happened to Lulu?*

What has happened to Lulu, mother?
  What has happened to Lu?
There's nothing in her bed but an old rag-doll
  And by its side a shoe.

Why is her window wide, mother,
  The curtain flapping free,
And only a circle on the dusty shelf
  Where her money-box used to be?

Why do you turn your head, mother,
  And why do the tear-drops fall?
And why do you crumple that note on the fire
  And say it is nothing at all?

I woke to voices late last night,
  I heard an engine roar.
Why do you tell me the things I heard
  Were a dream and nothing more?

I heard somebody cry, mother,
  In anger or in pain,
But now I ask you why, mother,
  You say it was a gust of rain?

Why do you wander about as though
  You don't know what to do?
What has happened to Lulu, mother?
  What has happened to Lu?

(Charles Causley)

► ## *She's Leaving Home*

Wednesday morning at 5 o'clock as the day begins,
silently closing her bedroom door,
leaving the note that she hoped would say more,
she goes downstairs to the kitchen,
clutching her handkerchief,
quietly turning the backdoor key,
stepping outside she is free.

⟫→

She (We gave her most of our lives)
is leaving (Sacrificed most of our lives)
home (We gave her everything money could buy)
She's leaving home after living alone
for so many years. Bye, Bye.
Father snores as his wife gets into her dressing-gown,
picks up the letter that's lying there,
standing alone at the top of the stairs,
she breaks down and cries to her husband:
'Daddy our baby's gone.
Why should she treat us so thoughtlessly?
How could she do this to me?'
She (We never thought of ourselves)
is leaving (Never a thought for ourselves)
home (We struggled hard all our lives to get by)
she's leaving home after living alone
for so many years. Bye, bye.
Friday morning at nine o'clock she is far away,
waiting to keep the appointment she made,
meeting a man from the motor trade.
She (What did we do that was wrong)
is having (We didn't know it was wrong)
fun (Fun is the one thing that money can't buy)
something inside that was always denied
for so many years. Bye, bye.
She's leaving home, bye bye.

(John Lennon/Paul McCartney)

☎ 2.   With your partner, write out the *events* which each poem
is describing. For example, in *What Has Happened to Lulu?*, first of
all Lulu took her money-box. Then she climbed through the window,
after ...

☎ 3.   What are the common features in each of the poems?
Make a list with your partner (e.g. both leave a note).

☎ 4.   Who is 'talking' in each poem? And what can we deduce
about the families in each case?

☎ 5.   What is the attitude of the mother in each of the poems?

☎ 6.   In *What Has Happened to Lulu?*

a) Notice that the writer uses 'do' a lot (e.g. 'Why do you turn your
   head ...?'). Usually we would use either 'are you turning' or 'have
   you turned'. With a partner, go through the poem re-writing the

lines where 'do' is used, to make them sound like everyday speech.
b) There are two things which give us a clue to Lulu's age. What are they?

🔑 7.   In *She's Leaving Home*, there are some lines which lead us to ask a number of questions. Work with a partner to try and answer these questions:

a) 'the note that she hoped would say more'. What do you think the note actually said? What more might she have said?
b) 'clutching her handkerchief'. Why is this detail mentioned? Can you guess what it implies?
c) 'after living alone for so many years'. What does this mean? We know she has been living with her parents.
d) 'our baby's gone'. What does this tell us about the mother's attitude to her daughter?
e) 'how could she do this to *me*'. Why not 'to *us*'? What does it reveal about the mother?
f) 'We never thought of ourselves'. Do you think this is true?
g) 'We didn't know it was wrong'. Is this really so? And *what* was 'wrong'?
h) 'something inside that was always denied'. What do you think this 'something' was?
i) The poem starts on Wednesday at 5 am and ends on Friday at 9 am. What do you suppose she did in the meantime?

Now change partners and compare your answers.

8.   Which of these two poems do you prefer? Write the title down together with your reasons. Then compare notes with a partner.

Writing

1.   Work in groups of four. First of all look at the notes you made in *Warming up* 1 and 2. Here you have a lot of sentences which describe the reasons for conflict between parents and their children. Try to combine them into a poem of about seven to eight lines beginning:

> Nothing I did was ever right ...

and ending

> Nothing they ever did was right.

Here is an example:

▶   Nothing I did was ever right:
         I never could stay out at night.
         They wouldn't let me watch TV,
         All they did was nag at me.
         They didn't like the friends I chose,
         And wouldn't let me choose my clothes.
         All we could do was row and fight –
         Nothing they ever did was right.

When you have finished, compare your poem with another group.

2. Work in pairs. Write the word CONFLICT vertically on a sheet of paper. Write a poem on the theme of conflict, each line of which starts with a letter of the word 'conflict'. For example:

         Can't you see that you're driving me
         Out of my mind with your
         Nonsense ...

3. Work in pairs. Go back to your notes in *Warming up* 3. Use these parental self-questionings to make sentences starting 'If only ...'

e.g.   If only I had been more tolerant.
         If only I had listened to her.
         etc.

Then combine these sentences in the most effective way possible to make a poem which starts:

         'If only' is a dream.

and the last line of which is:

         'If only' is a nightmare.

Compare your poem with another pair.

Reading alone

Here is a poem for you to read for yourself. Can you see the
relationship with the other two poems?

▶ *Sorry*

Dear parents,
I forgive you my life,
Begotten in a drab town,
The intention was good;
Passing the street now,
I see still the remains of sunlight.

It was not the bone buckled;
You gave me enough food
To renew myself.
It was the mind's weight
Kept me bent, as I grew tall.

It was not your fault.
What should have gone on,
Arrow aimed from a tried bow
At a tried target, has turned back,
Wounding itself
With questions you had not asked.

(R. S. Thomas)

4 Goodbyes

'Every time you say goodbye,
I die a little.'

How many goodbyes do we say in a lifetime? Most of the time it is a conventional formula when we leave someone. But when we are really saying goodbye, perhaps for the last time, to a friend, a lover, a dying person, then its meaning is reinforced.

Warming up

1.   Work in pairs to write down as many situations as possible when people say goodbye to each other. Then compare your list with another pair.
2.   Listen to the recording as you read the sentences below. After each one, try to work out what you think the situation was in which it was said (where it happened, who was speaking, to whom, what their relationship is, etc.). Remember, you can listen to the cassette more than once.

▶   'Well, it's getting late. I think we ought to be leaving, dear.'
'Goodnight. See you again on Saturday.'
'Well, I suppose it's time then. Goodbye.'
'Goodbye – and good luck to you both.'
'Goodbye Mum. I'll send you a postcard as soon as I get there.'
'Goodbye love. Take care. And don't forget to phone me when you arrive.'
'Goodbye then. Perhaps I'll see you again sometime.'
'Perhaps you'd better make a start now. I'll run you to the station.'
'This is it then at last. Goodbye.'

Compare your interpretations with a partner. If necessary check them by listening to the recording again.

Reading: Poem 1

1.   Read the poem *Goodbye*, as you listen to the recording. Do not worry about words you do not understand at this stage.

33

▶ ## *Goodbye*

So we must say Goodbye, my darling,
And go, as lovers go, for ever;
Tonight remains, to pack and fix on labels
And make an end of lying down together.

I put a final shilling in the gas,
And watch you slip your dress below your knees
And lie so still I hear your rustling comb
Modulate the autumn in the trees.

And all the countless things I shall remember
Lay mummy-cloths of silence round my head;
I fill the carafe with a drink of water;
You say 'We paid a guinea for this bed,'

And then, 'We'll leave some gas, a little warmth
For the next resident, and these dry flowers,'
And turn your face away, afraid to speak
The big word, that Eternity is ours.

Your kisses close my eyes and yet you stare
As though God struck a child with nameless fears;
Perhaps the water glitters and discloses
Time's chalice and its limpid useless tears.

Everything we renounce except our selves;
Selfishness is the last of all to go;
Our sighs are exhalations of the earth,
Our footprints leave a track across the snow.

We made the universe to be our home,
Our nostrils took the wind to be our breath,
Our hearts are massive towers of delight,
We stride across the seven seas of death.

Yet when all's done you'll keep the emerald
I placed upon your finger in the street;
And I will keep the patches that you sewed
On my old battledress tonight, my sweet.

(Alun Lewis)

Some of the words and phrases may need explanation:

fix on labels: attach cards to luggage with name and address on
a shilling in the gas: in some hotels and flats in Britain you have to
  put money into a box to make the gas fire work (a shilling = an old
  coin)
mummy-cloths: the cloths used to preserve bodies in Ancient Egypt
a guinea: an old coin (worth just over £1) no longer used
a chalice: a drinking cup
patches: the pieces of cloth soldiers have on their battledress to show
  their rank

2. Read this paraphrase of the poem:

'Goodbyes are terrible. We have to go through the trivial business
of packing, tying on labels and so on, while we know that our time
together is over. We have only one night together. I lie on the bed
as you undress and think of all the times we have spent together.
You say ordinary things about the room, and those who may use it
after us, but only to avoid the moment of eternity we shall now
spend. Our love is bigger than everything else, yet we know it must
end perhaps forever. But whatever happens, you will treasure the
ring I gave you, and I will treasure the badges you sewed on my
uniform before I go to war.'

3. Who is speaking in the poem? And who is the person
spoken to? Can you improve the paraphrase?
4. Read the poem over to yourself and note down the
rhyming lines. Use a, b, c, etc. as in the example on p. 19. Is the
rhyming scheme a regular one?

Reading: Poem 2

1. Read the poem *At Parting* as you listen to the recording.

▶ *At Parting*

> Since we through war awhile must part
> Sweetheart, and learn to lose
> Daily use
> Of all that satisfied our heart:
> Lay up those secrets and those powers
> Wherewith you pleased and cherished me these two years.

Now we must draw, as plants would,
On tubers stored in a better season,
Our honey and heaven;
Only our love can store such food.
Is this to make a god of absence?
A new-born monster to steal our sustenance?

We cannot quite cast out lack and pain.
Let him remain – what he may devour
We can well spare:
He never can tap this, the true vein.
I have no words to tell you what you were,
But when you are sad, think, Heaven could give no more.

(Anne Ridler)

Some words or phrases may need explanation:

awhile: for a time
lay up: put in store
wherewith: with which
tubers: the swollen root of a plant which stores its food
tap: to draw off the liquid from

2. Read the two poems again. Then discuss these points with a partner:
– why the couples have to part;
– how long their separation will last;
– how they feel about their separation.

3. Read these two paraphrases of *At Parting*:
'War is about to separate us, so we have to put to one side all the good things we have shared for the past two years. We shall have to rely on memories of our love. There is no way we can avoid the pain of absence but we have so much love in store that we should not regret it. Absence can never take away what we have had together, which was perfect.'

'This parting means we have to learn to live without each other for a time. We shall have to draw upon the store of happy memories of the past two years. I think of absence like an enormous creature trying to steal from our store. But there is no need to worry, since he can never steal the essential thing, which is our true love. If ever you feel sad, remember that what we have enjoyed was perfection.'

Which of them is the best account of the poem? Discuss your ideas with a partner. Can you improve your choice?

🔑 4.   Does *At Parting* rhyme? Use the letters a, b, c, etc. to mark the lines which rhyme, as in the example on p. 19. Are there any words which almost rhyme? Check your notes with a partner.

5.   Which poem do you prefer? Compare your preference with a partner.

Writing

1.   Work in groups of four. Write the word GOODBYE vertically on a sheet of paper. Each person in the group takes it in turn to give a word beginning with each of the letters of 'goodbye', e.g. g – goodbye, o – orchard, o – old, etc.

You should not think long before giving the word – any word will do as long as it starts with the right letter.

You should now try to construct a seven-line poem on the subject of parting. Each line must contain the corresponding word, though it need not be the first word in the line.

Here is an example:

▶
> We must say *g*oodbye
> To the *O*rchard where we played,
> To the *O*ld barn where we hid,
> To the *d*oor
> Which we close *b*ehind us now,
> On the *y*ard
> Where we lived our *e*arly years.

When you have finished, compare your poem with another group.

2.   Look back at *Warming up* 2. Work in groups of three. Take one of the parting lines and use it to try to make up a short four-line verse.

Here is an example:

▶
> 'I suppose it's time then.'
> 'Please don't go.'
> 'But really I must.'
> 'Can't you just say "no"?'

When you have finished it, try speaking the verse as a group. Clap your hands in time to the rhythm. If it does not quite fit, make changes in the poem until it does. Then recite your poem as a group for another group.

3.   Work in groups of four. First of all work together to write down all the different ways of saying 'goodbye' (e.g. goodbye, farewell, etc.). Who uses these words, and when? Each person in the group should choose one of the parting words and write a line on this pattern: 'Xs say Y and Z'. For example: '*Sons* say "*goodbye*" and *go*.' '*Old friends* say "*so long*" and *move away*.'

Then the group should arrange the lines in the best order to form a poem, making changes where necessary to improve on the sense, the rhythm or the rhyme.

When you have finished, compare your version with another group.

4.   In groups of four write down as many words as possible which describe parting (e.g. leaving, going, etc.). Write them in the *-ing* form.

Then write down adjectives you associate with parting (e.g. painful, gloomy, upsetting, etc.).

Then combine the nouns and adjectives in as many different ways as possible to form a rhythmic chant. It must have a strong rhythm. Here is an example:

►   Painful parting
            lonely leaving
            gloomy going
            frantic fleeing
            lonely going
            frantic parting
            gloomy leaving
            painful fleeing.
               (and so on with other combinations)

When you have finished, recite your poem as a group for another group.

Reading alone

Here is a poem for you to read on your own.

► *Goodbye*

'Don't lie' she said.
'I try' he said.
'My eye!' she said.
'Don't cry' he said.
'I'll die' she said.
'Oh my!' he said.
'Goodbye!' she said.

(Alan Maley)

5　What happened?

People fall in love. Then one day, circumstances change, or one of the partners behaves badly to the other, or interests diverge, or the magic is suddenly gone. And the partners are left to wonder what happened.

Warming up

1.　Read these two extracts.

> At that moment I thought she seemed more wonderful than ever; and then as she moved with final restlessness by the window I could bear it no longer and I said:
>
> 'I've got something to ask you. I've asked Juley but I haven't asked Bertie yet.' Now at last when I said it my voice seemed flat and strained. 'Would you marry me?'

She did not answer for a moment; she looked sideways with deep black eyes through the window. Across the lawns people were calling 'Good night' to each other. I could hear their voices rising after a silence of the strings.

Then she said: 'No.'

'Lydia—'

'I don't think I could,' she said.

From the back of my head delirium began to pound at me again.

'Oh! but my God,' I said. 'You've got to. I want so much—you've got to—'

'I haven't got to do anything.'

I could not speak. Outside, across the lawn, the orchestra did not begin again. In the silence I stood there still holding her.

I looked at her face, but she did not look at me, and I stared down at the small ear-ring box between her breasts. The orchestra still did not begin again and presently I said what, I suppose, everybody says at these times:

'Will you think it over? Will you think about it?'

'Of course I shall think about it,' she said. 'It's the first time—'

'Don't you love me any more?' I said.

'Love you?' she said. 'I don't know.'

'Would you kiss me?' I said.

She lifted her lips and I felt I achieved something, sterile though it was, as I kissed their unresponsive flatness. Then at last, down below, the orchestra started up again, making her break away.

'Let me go now,' she said.

'Don't go,' I said. 'Lydia, please don't go—'

I held her for a few moments longer; and then it occurred to me what the orchestra were playing. People were singing too.

'For she's a jolly good fellow – for she's a jolly good fellow – which nobody can deny –'

'Let me go,' she said. 'Let me go – they're singing for me.'

I opened my arms, letting her go. She sprang away from me, shaking her hair. With bitterness I said:

'You're twenty-one now. You can please yourself now, of course – it's all yours.'

She went out of the room, not speaking. I heard her running downstairs. I stood by the window and did not go after her . . . .

(H. E. Bates, *Love for Lydia*)

Louise said, 'I've known it for years. You don't love me.' She spoke with calm. He knew that calm – it meant they had reached the quiet centre of the storm: always in this region at about this time they began to speak the truth at each other. The truth, he thought, has never been of any real value to any human being – it is a symbol for mathematicians and philosophers to pursue. In human relations kindness and lies are worth a thousand truths. He involved himself in what he always knew was a vain struggle to retain the lies. 'Don't be absurd, darling. Who do you think I love if I don't love you?'

'You don't love anybody.'

'Is that why I treat you so badly?' He tried to hit a light note, and it sounded hollowly back at him.

'That's your conscience,' she said, 'your sense of duty. You've never loved anyone since Catherine died.'

'Except myself, of course. You always say I love myself.'

'No, I don't think you do.'

He defended himself by evasions. In this cyclonic centre he was powerless to give the comforting lie. 'I try all the time to keep you happy. I work hard for that.'

'Ticki, you won't even say you love me. Go on. Say it once.'

He eyed her bitterly over the pink gin, the visible sign of his failure: the skin a little yellow with atabrine, the eyes bloodshot with tears. No man could guarantee love for ever, but he had sworn fourteen years ago, at Ealing, silently, during the horrible little elegant ceremony among the lace and candles, that he would at least always see to it that she was happy.

'Ticki, I've got nothing except you, and you've got – nearly everything.' The lizard flicked across the wall and came to rest again, the wings of a moth in

his small crocodile jaws. The ants struck tiny muffled
blows at the electric globe.
    'And yet you want to go away from me,' he said.
    'Yes,' she said, 'I know you aren't happy either.
Without me you'll have peace.'

(Graham Greene, *The Heart of the Matter*)

2. How old do you think the people are in each extract? Which
of them wishes to stop the relationship? What are their reasons?
Discuss your answers with a partner.

3. Write down three of the main reasons people have for falling
out of love. Then compare your reasons in groups of four. Do you all
agree?

▶ 🔑 4. Listen to the people being interviewed on the recording. Make notes on what each one says about 'what happened'. Then
compare your notes with a partner. Remember, you can listen to the
cassette more than once.

Person	What happened?
Woman 1	
Woman 2	
Man	

Reading: Poems 1 and 2

1. Read these two poems as you listen to the recording.

▶ *I'm Looking Through You*

I'm looking through you,
where did you go?
I thought I knew you,
what did I know?
You don't look different, but you have changed,
I'm looking through you, you're not the same.
Your lips are moving,
I cannot hear,
your voice is soothing
but the words aren't clear.
You don't sound different, I've learnt the game,
I'm looking through you, you're not the same.
Why, tell me why did you not treat me right?
Love has a nasty habit of disappearing overnight,
you're thinking of me
the same old way,
you were above me,
but not today.
The only difference is you're down there.
I'm looking through you and you're nowhere.
Why, tell me why did you not treat me right?
Love has a nasty habit of disappearing overnight,
I'm looking through you,
where did you go?
I thought I knew you,
what did I know?
You don't look different, but you have changed,
I'm looking through you, you're not the same.
Yeh, I tell you you've changed.

(John Lennon/Paul McCartney)

▶ *Reported Missing*

Can you give me a precise description?
Said the policeman. Her lips, I told him,
Were soft. Could you give me, he said, pencil

Raised, a simile? Soft as an open mouth,
I said. Were there any noticeable
Peculiarities? he asked. Her hair hung
Heavily, I said. Any particular
Colour? he said. I told him I could recall
Little but its distinctive scent. What do
You mean, he asked, by distinctive? It had
The smell of a woman's hair, I said. Where
Were you? he asked. Closer than I am to
Anyone at present, I said; level with
Her mouth, level with her eyes. Her eyes?
He said. What about her eyes? There were two,
I said, both black. It has been established,
He said, that eyes cannot, outside common
Usage, be black; are you implying that
Violence was used? Only the gentle
Hammer blow of her kisses, the scent
Of her breath, the ... Quite, said the policeman,
Standing, but I regret that we know of
No one answering to such a description.

(Barry Cole)

2. *I'm Looking Through You*

a) The words are all quite commonly used ones. Are there any you
do not know? If so, try to work out what they mean. Then check
your guess against a dictionary.

b) There is an idiom in English: 'to *look through* someone'. Usually
it means that one person looks at another person, whom he or she
knows, but purposely does not 'see' or notice them. There is
another idiom 'to *see through* someone/something'. This means
to understand the motives (usually unpleasant) of another person.

Read the poem to yourself again. Then discuss how it fits these
two idioms.

c) Read these three possible paraphrases of the poem. Which one do
you think is the most accurate? Compare your ideas with a
partner. Can you improve on the paraphrase you have chosen?

You look exactly as you did before but my opinion of you has
changed because you did something mean, which hurt me.

When I look at you, I suddenly realise that I don't love you any
more. I can't understand why. Perhaps it's because I've grown
up, and you have stayed the same ('down there').

⟫⟫→

Your appearance is the same as before but, because of your recent behaviour, I don't admire you any more. I despise you.

d) How many of the lines are repeated in the poem? Which ones? Is there a pattern in these repetitions? In fact these are the words of a song. Does this help you to understand the purpose of the repetitions?

3. *Reported Missing*

a) Try to work out for yourself the meanings of the following words or phrases. Then compare your ideas with a partner. Only then consult a dictionary.

a simile, outside common usage, implying, a black eye, answering to such a description

b) This poem reads almost like a piece of prose, with some direct speech and some indirect speech. How do we know that it is a poem? Write down three things which signal to us that it is a poem. Then compare notes with a partner.

c) Which do you think is the best 'explanation' for the poem? When you have chosen, discuss your choice with a partner.

The poet is describing an actual event, when he got parted from his girlfriend in a crowd one day. He then reported his girlfriend's disappearance to a policeman.

The poet's girlfriend has just left him. He is remembering all her most attractive features. Because this is painful for him, he turns it into a kind of joke by imagining the incident with the policeman.

The poet wants to make a contrast between the literal mind of the policeman, who takes everything seriously, and the typical mind of a lover, whose head is filled with the images of his girlfriend.

4. Which of these two poems do you prefer? Can you justify your choice to a partner who has chosen differently?

Writing

1. Work in groups of four. Check on your notes for *Warming up* 4. You should have a number of sentences which people used to explain 'what happened' and why it happened. In your group, try to use these sentences to form a poem. You can either simply arrange the lines in the most satisfying order, or you can change and add to them if you prefer.

When you have finished, compare your poem with another group.

2. Work in groups of six. Each group member is given one of these verbs to work with: feel, remember, wonder, hope, know, try. The group will then write a poem starting with the line:

> 'Now you are gone,'

Each person uses his or her verb to write a sentence to complete this ...

> e.g.   Now you are gone,
> I wonder where you are.
> I know ... etc.

The group then decides how best to arrange these sentences to form a poem, and writes a good final punch line. (A 'punch line' is a very forceful, impressive last line.)

3. Work with a partner to discuss the kinds of questions you would need to ask to obtain a good description of someone.

> e.g.   What colour eyes does he have?
> How tall ...? etc.

Write out as many of these questions as you can. Then compare your ideas with another pair of students.

All four of you should now try to write a poem similar to *Reported Missing*. Begin with the line:

> 'Can you give me a precise description?'

Then use the ideas you have written down to write the questions. You will also need to find the answers (which can be humorous if you like, e.g. ' "What colour were her eyes?" he asked? "Pink," I replied'). You will also need to supply the reporting words, either in direct, or indirect speech, or in a mixture of both.

When you have finished, compare your poem with another group.

Reading alone

Here is a poem for you to read on your own.

► *Present Continuous*

Well, I am still
The unofficial guardian of your house,
Which is not your house any more
And not the same place we trusted to be there
Whenever we came home.

Our possessions lie
Abandoned, back along the way:
These books, those dresses under cellophane.
I haven't moved
Your plastic carrier bags from the hall
And fifty pairs of shoes
Still hang around the window on the stairs,
The changing fashions of your years with me.

(Hugo Williams)

6 It's mine...

When we go into someone's room or home for the first time, we are inevitably curious about the things in it. Things give an atmosphere and a character to places. Quite often we make assumptions about a person's character based on the appearance of their home and the kinds of things in it. And others certainly do the same about us!

Warming up

1. Make a list of three of your personal possessions which a friend, coming to your home for the first time, might notice.

When you are ready, exchange your list with a partner. Try to interpret your partner's character from his or her list (e.g. likes, dislikes, habits, etc.). Does your partner agree with your interpretation?

2. Read these two short passages. Then, in groups of three, discuss:

– who do you think lives there (a man, a woman, young, old, married or not, etc.);

– what sort of a person they are.

Compare your answers with another group.

▶ That kitchen, worn by our boots and lives, was scruffy, warm, and low, whose fuss of furniture seemed never the same but was shuffled around each day. A black grate crackled with coal and beech-twigs; towels toasted on the guard; the mantel was littered with fine old china, horse brasses, and freak potatoes. On the floor were strips of muddy matting, the windows were choked with plants, the walls supported stopped clocks and calendars, and smoky fungus ran over the ceilings. There were also six tables of different sizes, some armchairs gapingly stuffed, boxes, stools and unravelling baskets, books and papers on every chair, a sofa for cats, a harmonium for coats, and a piano for dust and photographs. These were the shapes of our kitchen landscape, the rocks of our submarine life, each object worn smooth by our constant nuzzling, or encrusted by lively barnacles, relics of birthdays and dead relations, wrecks of furniture long since foundered, all silted deep by Mother's newspapers which the years piled round on the floor.

(Laurie Lee, *Cider with Rosie*)

▶ The room was as curious as its occupant. It looked like a small museum. It was both broad and deep, with cupboards and cabinets all round, crowded with specimens, geological and anatomical. Cases of butterflies and moths flanked each side of the entrance. A large table in the centre was littered with all sorts of debris, while the tall brass tube of a powerful microscope bristled up amongst them. As I glanced round I was surprised at the universality of the man's interests. Here was a case of ancient coins. There was a cabinet of flint instruments. Behind his central table was a large cupboard of fossil bones. Above was a line of plaster skulls with such names as 'Neander-thal', 'Heidelberg', 'Cromagnon' printed beneath them.

(Sir Arthur Conan Doyle, *The Adventure of the Three Garridebs*)

3.   Try to decide what is your most treasured object. Why is this object so valuable to you? Make some brief notes.

Then work with a partner and explain to him or her why you treasure this object so much.

Reading: Poem 1

1.   Read this poem as you listen to the recording.

▶ *The Rag Doll to the Heedless Child*

I love you
with my linen heart.

You cannot
know how these

rigid, lumpy arms
shudder in your grasp,

or what
tears dam up against

these blue eye-smudges at
your capriciousness.

At night I watch you sleep;
you'll never know

how I thrust my face
into the stream

of your warm breath;
and how

love-words choke me behind
this sewn-up mouth.

(David Harsent)

Some words and phrases may need some explanation:

heedless: uncaring
linen: a type of thick fabric/cloth
shudder: a shaking or shivering movement caused by fear, strong
   emotion or cold
grasp: a strong hold or grip with the hand
dam up: are held back and build up in volume
capriciousness: unpredictable behaviour
thrust: push strongly against something
choke: suffocate

2.   Make a list of all the words in the poem which reveal the identity of the speaker. Compare your list with a partner.

3.   Look at this picture of a child and a doll.

Work in the same groups of five. Use the following verbs: read, speak, explain, touch, hear. Each member of the group should use one verb to complete this pattern:

If only I could ... (*verb*)
I would ...

(The 'I' in the sentence is the rag doll.)
Here is an example:

If only I could *read*
I would *look over your shoulder.*

When all five sentences are ready, the group should combine them in the best order to make a poem. You can make minor alterations and improvements if you like.

Compare your poem with another group.

Reading: Poem 2

1. Read *Boy at the Window* as you listen to the recording.

▶ ## Boy at the Window

Seeing the snowman standing all alone
In dusk and cold is more than he can bear.
The small boy weeps to hear the wind prepare
A night of gnashings and enormous moan.
His tearful sight can hardly reach to where
The pale-faced figure with bitumen eyes
Returns him such a god-forsaken stare
As outcast Adam gave to Paradise.

The man of snow is, nonetheless, content,
Having no wish to go inside and die.
Still, he is moved to see the youngster cry.
Though frozen water is his element,
He melts enough to drop from one soft eye
A trickle of the purest rain, a tear
For the child at the bright pane surrounded by
Such warmth, such light, such love, and so much fear.

(Richard Wilbur)

Here are the meanings of some of the words and expressions:

gnashings: the sound your teeth make when you grind them together
bitumen: tar (or coal)
a god-forsaken stare: a lonely expression
outcast Adam ... Paradise: Adam was the first man God created (in
    the Bible). Paradise was heaven, the perfect world. Adam and his
    wife, Eve, were thrown out of Paradise when they ate the apple of
    the tree of knowledge.
a trickle: a small flow of water
a pane: a window

🔑 2. Read the first verse of the poem again. With a partner try
to decide:
a) who 'he' refers to in line 2;
b) who 'his' refers to in line 5;
c) who 'him' refers to in line 7;
d) who 'the pale-faced figure' is in line 6.
   3. Try to find one word to summarise the feelings of the boy, and
another for those of the snowman.
   Compare your words with a partner.
🔑 4. Read the second verse again. The structure is quite
complicated, with a number of key changes of direction: *nonetheless,
still, though* ...
   Try to write out this verse in ordinary language but using different
linking words. For example:
          '*However*, the snowman is quite pleased, *since* ...'   or
          '*Despite* what the boy thinks, the snowman ...'
Compare your version with a partner.
🔑 5. Write out the rhyme scheme of the poem using the letters
a, b, c, etc., as in the example on p. 19.
   6. Why does the poet write 'and so much fear' at the end of the
poem? What exactly does it mean? Fear of what? Try to explain this
line to a partner.
   7. Which poem did you enjoy most? Can you explain your
reasons to a partner?

Writing

   1. Think back to *Warming up 3* – your most treasured object. In
particular think about:

– how you acquired it;
– when you got it;
– where it came from;
– who sold or gave it to you;
– where you keep it;
– what you do with it;
– why you value it so much.

Write some notes in answer to these points. Then try to write a short poem using this information. Write it as if the object was speaking (use 'I') to 'you' (the owner).

Here is an example:

▶ ## *The Pocket Watch*

Although I am a pocket watch
My hands are now too weak
To tell the time.
For I am old
And cannot speak.
I am not worth a dime.
You keep me now
For old time's sake
But every time I hear the hours chime
My heart would break.

2.   Divide the letters of the alphabet roughly equally between groups. For example if there are five groups of five, Group 1 would have A to E, Group 2, F to J, and so on.

In each group each person writes down five objects, each one beginning with one of the five letters given to the group. (For example, a person in Group 1 might write Apple, Box, Car, Doll, Egg.)

The group then compares its lists.

Each member has five items beginning with the same five letters. From these the group has to choose the 'best' five – one for each letter. These five words are then arranged in the best rhythmical order, and finished off with a final line:

Verse 1   . . . sit upon the sill.
Verse 2   . . . stand upon the shelf.
Verse 3   . . . lie upon the ledge.
Verse 4   . . . pile up on the parquet.
Verse 5   . . . cascade on the carpet.

It's mine . . .

So Group 1 might make a verse like this example:

Apples, boxes, cars,
Dolls and broken eggs
Sit upon the sill.

Notice that it will sometimes be necessary to put in an adjective, like 'broken', to keep the rhythm going.

When all groups have finished writing their verse, the whole alphabet poem can be recited group by group.

Reading alone

Here is a poem to read for yourself.

▶ *Two Clocks*

There was a clock in Grandad's house:
black, gold-numbered,
and a three-foot pendulum.
I'd hear it tick out endless Christmasses,

Such splendour. *His* chair.
His knife. *His* fork. 'Wait!'
Grandma would say,
' 'til your father gets in!'
Twisting my mother to a girl again.

Revenge needs time. 'That junk,'
my mother said,
and burned the clock,
the velvet, the Blessed Are the Pure in Heart
in red and gold behind the bed.

And brought him back to live with us,
where bleak electric hands swirled gently,
slicing her days and his
into thin fragments.

(John Daniel)

7 Nonsense!

In America people die of overeating; in Africa they starve to death.
Some countries expel citizens who have the 'wrong' beliefs, others

refuse to let them go. Some people are born to riches but fail to enjoy them. Others have little but enjoy what they have. DDT, which saves us from plant pests, also poisons us and our food. The world is an absurd place where we can rely on nothing except arbitrary nonsense. So why should not poetry reflect some of that nonsense?

Warming up

1. Look at the picture on p. 57. What does it mean?

2. Read this rhyme.

► ## A Traditional Rhyme

One fine day in the middle of the night,
Two dead men got up to fight.
Back to back they faced each other,
Drew their swords and shot each other.
A paralysed donkey passing by
Kicked a blind man in the eye,
Knocked him through a nine-inch wall
Into a dry ditch and drowned them all.

This is a children's rhyme which is still recited in school playgrounds. Do you know any other rhymes like this, either in English or in your own language?
What is the function of rhymes like this?

Reading: Poems 1 and 2

1. Read these two poems as you listen to the recording.

► ## Tonight at Noon

Tonight at noon
Supermarkets will advertise 3d EXTRA on everything
Tonight at noon
Children from happy families will be sent to live in a home
Elephants will tell each other human jokes
America will declare peace on Russia
World War I generals will sell poppies in the streets on
        November 11th

The first daffodils of autumn will appear
When the leaves fall upwards to the trees

Tonight at noon
Pigeons will hunt cats through city backyards
Hitler will tell us to fight on the beaches and on the landing fields
A tunnel full of water will be built under Liverpool
Pigs will be sighted flying in formation over Woolton
     and Nelson will not only get his eye back but his arm as well
White Americans will demonstrate for equal rights in front of
    the Black House
and the Monster has just created Dr Frankenstein

Girls in bikinis are moonbathing
Folksongs are being sung by real folk
Art galleries are closed to people over 21
Poets get their poems in the Top 20
Politicians are elected to insane asylums
There's jobs for everyone and nobody wants them
In back alleys everywhere teenage lovers are kissing in broad
    daylight

In forgotten graveyards everywhere the dead will quietly bury
    the living
And
You will tell me you love me
Tonight at noon

(Adrian Henri)

There are many references to things you may not be familiar with:

3d EXTRA *on everything:* (3d in the old currency; now, after
    metrication, it would be 3p.) It is common in supermarkets for
    special bargains to be marked '3p (pence) off' (*not extra*)
a home: a hostel for children who come from broken homes, or who
    have no parents
elephants ... jokes: There was a fashion at the time the poem was
    written for telling jokes about elephants. (For example: How does
    an elephant get down from a tree? He waits for autumn and floats
    down on a leaf.)
poppies: artificial poppies are sold on 11 November in remembrance
    of those who died in the First World War
fight on the beaches: a quotation from a speech by Churchill in the
    Second World War (against Hitler)

a tunnel full of water ... under Liverpool: there is a real tunnel under
    the River Mersey in Liverpool (not full of water)
Woolton: part of Liverpool
the Black House: the White House – US President's residence
Dr Frankenstein: in Mary Shelley's famous book, Dr Frankenstein
    creates a monster
real folk: ordinary people
Top 20: the chart showing which songs are the most popular

▶   *Daydream*

> One day people will touch and talk perhaps easily,
> And loving be natural as breathing and warm as sunlight,
> And people will untie themselves, as string is unknotted,
> Unfold and yawn and stretch and spread their fingers,
> Unfurl, uncurl like seaweed returned to the sea,
> And work will be simple and swift as a seagull flying,
> And play will be casual and quiet as a seagull settling,
> And the clocks will stop, and no-one will wonder or care or
>   notice,
> And people will smile without reason, even in the winter, even in
>   the rain.

(A. S. J. Tessimond)

  2. *Tonight at Noon*
a) Which of these four interpretations of the poem do you think is
    best? Discuss your choice with a partner.

> Because you love me, the world has turned upside down and
> the strangest things can happen.

> It is as unlikely that you will tell me you love me, as that all
> these weird things will happen.

> If I could make all these strange things occur, perhaps you
> would love me.

> If you would only love me, then I am sure all these bizarre
> things would happen.

🗝 b) Try to write out the poem by reversing all the lines back to
    normal. For example, you would start like this:
        'Today at noon
        Supermarkets will advertise 3d off everything ...'

There will be some 'problem' lines. Discuss these with a partner or with your teacher.

3. *Daydream*

☛ a) The poet is contrasting what will happen 'one day' with what he believes is the situation today. Try to write out this present situation. You might start:

> 'As things are at present, people don't touch or talk to each other easily. They ...'

When you have finished, compare your version with a partner.

b) Do you agree with the writer's opinion?

☛ 4. What are the similarities between these two poems? And what is the major difference?

5. Which poem do you prefer? Try to explain your choice to a partner.

Writing

1. One way of producing an absurd piece of writing is by playing *Consequences*.

In groups of six, each person takes a piece of paper and writes the name of a boy/man and the word 'met' (e.g. Napoleon met). The paper is then folded to hide what has been written and passed to the next person. This time the name of a girl/woman is written, the paper folded and passed on again. Successively, the *place* of meeting, *what he said to her*, *what she said to him* and *the result* are written. Each person then unfolds the paper and reads the result.

Here is an example of what might result:

> Napoleon met
> Agatha Christie
> at the airport.
> He said, 'Stop fidgeting.'
> She said, 'I'd love a biscuit.'
> And in the end they decided to go to a disco.

2. Here is a variation of this. Work in pairs. One person is A, the other B. A writes the first half of a comparison with 'as' on the paper, then folds it and hands it to B (e.g. As rich as ...). B then writes the second half of the comparison – without knowing what the first half was. Here are some possible results:

As rich as an egg.
As beautiful as a frying pan.

Compare your results in groups of six. Try to compose a poem using the six absurd comparisons. You might start with the line:

'You're simply incomparable!'

and finish with the line:

'I told you you were incomparable!'

3. Work in groups of six. Three people will be As, the other three, Bs. The As each write two phrases on this pattern: 'The X will be full of ...' (e.g. The sea will be full of ...). The Bs all write two phrases on the adjective and noun pattern (e.g. delicious meals).

The group then decides on the best combinations of the A phrases and the B phrases, thus producing six sentences.

e.g.   The sea will be full of Easter eggs.
         The air will be full of chocolate cake.

These should be put together in the best order to form a poem. The group should decide on a good punch line to finish the poem off.

Reading alone

Here are two poems for you to read by yourself.

▶   There was a young lad from New York
         Who had an aversion to pork.
         If they served it at table,
         He just wasn't able
         to touch it with knife or with fork.

▶   There was a nice girl from Seattle
         Who unfortunately tended to prattle.
         Said her man from the East,
         'If this doesn't cease,
         I'll put you outside with the cattle.'

This kind of five-line humorous poem is called a *limerick* and is a very popular (disrespectful!) form of verse in English. The humour is often based on some kind of stereotype – cultural, sexual, etc. You might like to try to write a limerick yourself – start with the name of a place, e.g. 'There was a young man from Dundee,' then go on, keeping the rhythm and the rhyme as in the two examples.

8   Construction

Whenever men are digging a hole, or erecting a new building, a crowd will gather to watch. There is something endlessly fascinating about construction sites.

Warming up

1.   When you see a new building going up, what do you think of? Write down three things. Then compare your ideas in groups of four.

▶ ▬▬🔑   2.   Listen to the recording. You will hear people explaining what passes through their minds when they see a new block going up. Make careful notes, then compare them with a partner. Remember, you can listen to the cassette more than once.

Person	Feelings about new construction
Man 1	
Woman 1	
Woman 2	
Man 2	

Reading: Poems 1 and 2

1. Read these two poems as you listen to the recording.

► *Construction Site*

I look into the spaces where,
Going about their vacant geometry,
The cranes sketch theoretical
Apartments in the air.

And do our ghostly
Future counterparts
Regard us with, as yet, uncurtained eyes,
And simulate the symmetry of our hearts?

(Alan Maley)

Some words may need explanation:

cranes: big machines for lifting materials from one place to another
counterparts: people who play the same parts as ourselves

simulate: copy
symmetry: the same on one side as on the other

▶ ## *Scaffolding*

Masons, when they start upon a building,
Are careful to test out the scaffolding;

Make sure that planks won't slip at busy points,
Secure all ladders, tighten bolted joints.

And yet all this comes down when the job's done,
Showing off walls of sure and solid stone.

So if, my dear, there sometimes seem to be
Old bridges breaking between you and me

Never fear. We may let the scaffolds fall
Confident that we have built our wall.

(Seamus Heaney)

Some words may need explanation:

scaffolding: the framework workmen walk on to construct a building
masons: skilled men who build in stone

2. *Construction Site*

🗝️ a) Here is a brief explanation of the poem *Construction Site*. Use the words which follow to complete the blanks.

The .... is standing with the .... he
............................, looking out of the window of his own
.... at the .... site ....
He imagines the .... are drawing ....
in the .... of the .... which will later
be .... there. He goes on to ....
whether the ghosts of the .... who will
.... opposite are .... at them, and
whether their .... will be as much
.... as his with his lover's.

*people, apartments, cranes, apartment, pictures, built, looking,
live, air, construction, woman, opposite, loves, hearts, writer,
in tune, ask*

b) Do you agree with this interpretation? Can you improve on it?

c) Which word in the second verse reminds us of the 'geometrical' image in the first verse?

3. *Scaffolding*

a) Which of these paraphrases of the poem do you think is the better? Discuss your choice with a partner. Can you improve upon your choice?

> The writer reassures his lover by comparing their relationship with scaffolding and the finished building. Because they have built a solid wall of love, the small disagreements they have (the old bridges breaking) can be disregarded.

> The writer tells his lover not to worry if the things that first brought them together (the scaffolding) are being lost. They have now built a solid wall of more lasting interests.

4. Compare the two poems. What are the similarities between them? (There are two major similarities.)

5. Which poem did you prefer? Discuss your choice with a partner.

Writing

1. Work in groups of six. Each person is given one of these words: who, what, whether, why, where, how. Individually, write a sentence on this pattern: 'I wonder who (why, etc.) ...'. These six sentences are then put together in the best order to form a poem, the first two lines of which are:

> 'As I watch the building growing there
> In the vacant lot across the square'

Then the group as a whole should try and find a good punch line.

2. Again in groups of six, each person writes a phrase beginning 'someone who ...'. These are then arranged in the best order to form a poem beginning:

> 'Who knows? Perhaps in one of those
> Blank windows in the facing block
> Lives someone who ...'

For example:

> Who knows? Perhaps in one of those
> Blank windows in the facing block
> Lives someone who looks back at me;
> Someone who needs company;
> Someone who is crazy about jazz;
> Someone who would share the things he has.
>   etc.

Once again the whole group should write a good punch line to finish the poem off.

3.   Work in groups of four. Write the word BUILDING vertically on a sheet of paper. Group members take it in turns to think of a word beginning with each of these initial letters (e.g. b – behind, u – up, i – into, l – level). Do not think too long about the choice of word – any word will do so long as it starts with the appropriate letter.

The group then constructs an eight-line poem in which the words chosen must fit in the corresponding lines (they need not be the first word in each line).

Here is an example:

▶   *Behind* the house were fields,
      And higher *up* a wood
      Where we would play *into* the dusk,
      Until the builders came to *level* fields,
      Cut *down* the old familiar trees,
      And architects cancelled our paradise with *ink*.
      Sudden, *new*, unfamiliar shapes
      Loomed up, *grew* menacing overnight.

When you have finished compare your poem with another group.

Reading alone

1. Here is a poem for you to read by yourself.

► *Walking Tall*

Whenever I see
A new block go up,
I think of us as kids,
Impatient to grow;
How slow it seemed at first,
The others so far ahead,
Above –
Almost out of sight.
(Would we ever reach your height?)
Then, overnight,
There we were
Up there among the best of them,
And there we remain –
Stuck on the top
Of our separate buildings.

(Alan Maley)

2. If you have had a vivid experience connected with buildings or construction, try to write your own poem about it.

9 The takeover

Mankind has become so used to thinking of itself as the dominant species that we tend to forget that we are only one of the forms of life which could control our planet.

Warming up

1.   Suppose that mankind was suddenly annihilated, destroyed; which do you think would be the most likely species to take over? Write your opinion down. Then compare opinions in groups of four.

2.   Read the following extracts, then discuss them in pairs. Which do you think sounds the most likely?

▶   The smaller birds were at the window now. He recognised the light tap-tapping of their beaks, and the soft brush of their wings. The hawks ignored the windows. They concentrated their attack upon the door. Nat listened to the tearing sound of splintering wood, and wondered how many million years of memory were stored in those little brains, behind the stabbing beaks, the piercing eyes, now giving them this instinct to destroy mankind with all the deft precision of machines.

(Daphne du Maurier, *The Birds*)

▶   In sum, a full-scale nuclear attack on the United States would devastate the natural environment on a scale unknown since early geological times, when, in response to natural catastrophes whose nature has not been determined, sudden mass extinctions of species and whole ecosystems occurred all over the earth. How far this 'gross simplification' of the environment would go once virtually all animal life and the greater part of plant life had been destroyed and what patterns the surviving remnants of life would arrange themselves into over the long run are imponderables; but it appears that at the outset the United States would be a republic of insects and grass.

(Jonathan Schell, *The Fate of the Earth*)

Reading: Poems 1 and 2

1. Read these two poems as you listen to the recording.

▶ *Mushrooms*

Overnight, very
Whitely, discreetly,
Very quietly
Our toes, our noses
Take hold on the loam,
Acquire the air.

Nobody sees us,
Stops us, betrays us;
The small grains make room.

Soft fists insist on
Heaving the needles,
The leafy bedding,

Even the paving.
Our hammers, our rams,
Earless and eyeless,

Perfectly voiceless,
Widen the crannies,
Shoulder through holes. We

Diet on water,
On crumbs of shadow,
Bland-mannered, asking

Little or nothing.
So many of us!
So many of us!

We are shelves, we are
Tables, we are meek,
We are edible,

Nudgers and shovers
In spite of ourselves.
Our kind multiplies:

≫→

We shall by morning
Inherit the earth.
Our foot's in the door.

(Sylvia Plath)

Some words may need explanation:

loam: earth, soil
needles: pine needles
leafy bedding: the layer of leaves on top of the soil
rams: an instrument for breaking down doors, etc.
crannies: small cracks
bland-mannered: mild-mannered, very polite
meek: modest, mild
edible: eatable
nudgers: people who use their elbows to push others aside
shovers: people who push other people violently

► ## And the Flies will be Supreme

do you see them?
    there – there, in the bins . . .
buzzing, humming, flying round.
spreading filth, eating filth . . . Why are they there?
    they are biding their time.
    yes. they are biding their time,
preparing for the day that will come
    when the Flies will be supreme.

for when men are dead of heat and dust
the Flies will be supreme.
    that is why they live on . . . multiplying . . .
they are preparing, watching, waiting,
    waiting for the finger that will press the button.
    waiting for the buildings that will topple.
    waiting for the dust that will kill . . .
and the Flies will be supreme.
and the Flies will be supreme.

(Zoe Ann Fairbairns)

Some words may need explanation:

biding their time: waiting for their time to come
topple: fall down

2. *Mushrooms*

🗝 a) Make a list of all the words in the poem which express mildness (e.g. discreetly, very quietly, etc.). Check your list with a partner.

🗝 b) Make another list, this time of words which express the irresistible force of the mushrooms (e.g. take hold, make room, etc.). Check your list with your partner again.

3. *And the Flies will be Supreme*
a) Which of these two interpretations is the better?

> The flies are preparing for the day when men destroy themselves with nuclear weapons. Then they will take over.

> The flies are preparing themselves to take over from men, when mankind has ruined the environment, turning it into a hot, dry desert.

🗝 4. Look at the two poems again. How many similarities can you find between them? Check your ideas with a partner.

5. Which do you find is the more menacing? And which one do you prefer? Discuss your replies with your partner.

Writing

1. In pairs, write a poem with the title *The Animals*. The first lines should be:
> 'The day of the animals was at hand,
> And they came:'
And the last line:
> 'And the day of the animals had come.'

The words of the poem should be made up of the names of insects, animals and birds, four words to each line. So you should start by writing down as many animals' names as possible. Then try to arrange them in the best order. For example, the first lines might go like this:

> The day of the animals was at hand,
> And they came:
> Buffaloes, Bears, Blackbirds and Boars ...

2. Work in groups of four. Discuss the ideas you noted in *Warming up* 1. The group should first of all agree on *what* would be most likely to take over from mankind. Then each person in the group should write two short sentences which describe this takeover.

The group then looks at these eight sentences and tries to arrange them into a poem. If some of the sentences do not fit very well, discuss how to change them so that they do.

Finally, groups exchange poems, and make suggestions for further improvements, either by adding or changing lines.

3. This is a picture of a mosquito.

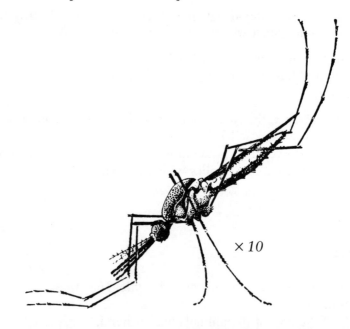

× 10

Imagine that, by a mutation, mosquitoes became the size of motor cars. What would the results be for mankind? First of all write down your own ideas, then compare them in groups of four.

Finally try to write them out in the form of a poem. It might begin:

> 'It was the noise we noticed first;
> Familiar somehow, but never so loud as this ...'

Reading alone

Here is a poem to read on your own.

► *Beleaguered Cities*

Build your houses, build your houses, build your towns,
    Fell the woodland, to a gutter turn the brook,
Pave the meadows, pave the meadows, pave the downs,
    Plant your bricks and mortar where the grasses shook,
    The wind-swept grasses shook.
Build, build your Babels black against the sky –
But mark yon small green blade, your stones between,
    The single spy
Of that uncounted host you have outcast;
For with their tiny pennons waving green
    They shall storm your streets at last.

Build your houses, build your houses, build your slums,
    Drive your drains where once the rabbits used to lurk,
Let there be no song there save the wind that hums
    Through the idle wires while dumb men tramp to work,
    Tramp to their idle work.
Silent the siege; none notes it; yet one day
Men from your walls shall watch the woods once more
    Close round their prey.
Build, build the ramparts of your giant-town;
Yet they shall crumble to the dust before
    The battering thistle-down.

(F. L. Lucas)

10   On reflection

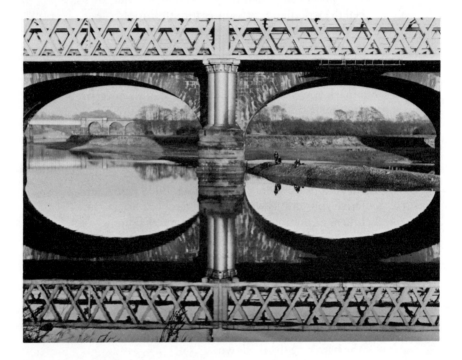

Things are not always what they seem. And especially when the world is turned upside-down in a reflection, familiar shapes can take on new and unusual identities.

Warming up

1. Look at the pictures on pp. 77 and 78. You can see the reflection but not what caused it. Try to work out:
- where it is (in which country);
- whether it is a scene in the city or the countryside;
- what time of year it might be;
- what objects, people, etc., you can see in the reflection.

a)

b)

c)

d)

Compare your ideas with a partner. Do you agree?

2. Take a square piece of white paper. Fold it down the middle. Then drop some black ink on the fold line, fold it over and press hard. Then open the paper again. You will have something like this:

With a partner discuss your ink-blots. What do the shapes remind you of? Try turning them sideways and upside down. Does this change your ideas?

3. Take a leaf from a tree, and fold it down the middle.

What do you notice?

There are many shapes in nature which are symmetrical like this. That is, one side of them is, in a way, reflected in the other side. With a partner try to think of as many natural symmetrical shapes as possible.

Reading: Poem 1

1. Read this poem as you listen to the recording. Do not worry if there are words you do not understand at first.

► *Water Picture*

In the pond in the park
all things are doubled:
Long buildings hang and
wriggle gently. Chimneys
are bent legs bouncing
on clouds below. A flag
wags like a fishhook
down there in the sky.

»»→

The arched stone bridge
is an eye, with underlid
in the water. In its lens
dip crinkled heads with hats
that don't fall off. Dogs go by,
barking on their backs.
A baby, taken to feed the
ducks, dangles upside down
a pink balloon for a buoy.

Treetops deploy a haze of
cherry bloom for roots,
where birds coast belly up
in the glass bowl of a hill;
from its bottom a bunch
of peanut-munching children
is suspended by their
sneakers, waveringly.

A swan, with twin necks
forming the figure three,
steers between two dimpled
towers doubled. Fondly
hissing, she kisses herself,
and all the scene is troubled:
water-windows splinter,
tree-limbs tangle, the bridge
folds like a fan.

(May Swenson)

2.   There are some words and expressions which may be unfamiliar. Work in groups of about four. Half the groups should study the glosses for verses 1 and 2. The other groups will be responsible for looking up the additional words (see p. 87). Groups then exchange information. For verses 3 and 4, groups reverse roles. Those who studied the glosses will look up the additional words (see p. 87), and vice versa.

Verses 1 and 2 – Glosses

doubled: repeated
wriggle: twist about like a worm or a snake
bouncing: hitting a surface and springing back again

arched: curved
underlid: the bottom edge of an eye
lens: usually glass for enlarging objects (e.g. in a camera), here it
   refers to the part of the eye we see through

Verses 3 and 4 – Glosses

deploy: spread out
haze: a fine mist
coast: move smoothly along without effort
steers: directs its way, guides itself
dimpled: with small hollows in them
splinter: break up into small fragments

⚷ 3.   The things reflected in the water take on a new appearance. The poet compares them with a number of different things. Go
through the poem again and note down the comparisons she makes.
The first one has been done for you.

Object	*Comparison*
chimneys	bent legs
flag	
arched stone bridge	
pink balloon	
cherry bloom	
a hill	
a swan	
the bridge	

Compare your notes with a partner.

⚷ 4.   The poet often uses metaphor to express her meaning
more vividly. For example, when she writes:
      'Long buildings hang and wriggle gently'
we can more easily see the image she wishes to create in our mind's
eye. The buildings do seem to hang upside down in the water, almost
like clothes hanging on a line. And the movement of the water does
make them *wriggle* like snakes. Of course, we would not usually use
'hang' or 'wriggle' with 'building', but this unusual combination
creates a powerful and effective image.
   Can you find other examples in the poem where verbs are used
metaphorically? Make a list and compare it with a partner. For a

more detailed explanation of what is meant by metaphor, look at p. 105.

5. This is a poem which does not rhyme. Instead, the poet uses the repetition of sounds to create a poetic effect (e.g. p̲ond in the park and fl̲ag wag̲s).

Go through the poem with a partner underlining repeated consonants and vowels. Then compare your notes with another pair.

Reading: Poem 2

1. Read this poem as you listen to the recording.

► *The Waterglass*

A church tower crowned the town,
double in air and water,
and over anchored houses
the round bells rolled at noon.
Bubbles rolled to the surface.
The drowning bells swirled down.

A sun burned in the bay.
A lighthouse towered downwards,
moored in the mirroring fathoms.
The seaweed swayed its tree.
A boat below me floated
upside down on the sky.

An underwater wind
ruffled the red-roofed shallows,
where wading stilt-legged children
stood in the clouded sand,
and down from the knee-deep harbour
a ladder led to the drowned.

Gulls fell out of the day.
The thrown net met its image
in the window of the water.
A ripple slurred the sky.
My hand swam up to meet me,
and I met myself in the sea.

Mirrored, I saw my death
in the underworld in the water,
and saw my drowned face sway in
the glass day underneath –
till I spoke to my speaking likeness,
and the moment broke with my breath.

(Alistair Reid)

2. Work in groups of four. Some groups will be A groups, others B groups. A groups will be responsible for finding the meanings of new words in verses 1 and 2, B groups for verses 3 and 4. All groups will check on new words in verse 5. Some of the glosses have been done for you:

Verse 1

crowned: stood on the top of
anchored:
swirled:

Verse 2

moored: fastened with a rope to the shore
fathoms:
seaweed:
swayed: moved gently from side to side

Verse 3

ruffled: disturbed
shallows:
wading:
stilt-legged: as if walking on stilts (long poles which act as a way of
  lengthening the legs)

Verse 4

gulls:
a ripple:
slurred: blurred, made marks on

Verse 5

likeness: resemblance

⚿ 3. Note down all the words in the poem which are associated with the sea. Compare notes with a partner.

In some cases these sea words are used in unexpected combinations. For example, 'anchored houses'. We would expect ships to be anchored, not houses.

Try to find *five* more examples of unusual combinations of adjective and noun. In each case write out a more usual combination (e.g. for 'anchored houses' you might write 'anchored ships').

When you have finished compare your list with a partner.

⚿ 4. *The Waterglass* contains other examples of unusual ways of using words. For example:

'A lighthouse towered downwards'.

Things usually tower upwards, not downwards.

With a partner look at the following examples:
– The seaweed swayed its tree.'
– 'A boat below me floated
  upside down on the sky.'
– 'Gulls fell out of the day.'
– 'A ripple slurred the sky.'
– 'My hand swam up to meet me.'
Try to re-write each of these lines to show in more ordinary language what the writer meant. For example:

The seaweed swayed like a tree.

⚿ 5. Does this poem rhyme? Note down any rhymes you can find and compare them with a partner.

There are many examples of repeated consonant and vowel sounds in this poem too. Work with your partner to note as many of them as possible (e.g. <u>b</u>urned in the <u>b</u>ay, <u>tow</u>er cr<u>ow</u>ned the <u>tow</u>n).

⚿ 6. In both poems there is a similar pattern: first a description of the reflection, then a break up of the picture. What causes the shattering of the picture in each poem? Can you write out the lines which describe it?

7. Which poem did you prefer? Try to explain your reasons to a partner.

Writing

1. Look carefully at the picture opposite with a partner. Imagine how the picture would look if it were reflected in water. (In *Water*

Picture for example, the chimneys looked like bent legs, the flag like a fishhook.)

Make a list of all the things in the picture and the comparisons their reflections might generate.

Then compare your lists in groups of four, and arrange the best ideas into a poem beginning with the line:

'In the water's face I see ...'

and ending:

'Things are seldom what they seem to be.'

2. Imagine that you are standing in front of a mirror which, quite suddenly, shatters. What would you see? What would you feel?

Write down all the things that come to mind immediately. They could be reflections you see in the broken glass or thoughts about the shattered mirror. (For example: One eye thrown to the floor, the other to the ceiling. A nose split into two. A smile transformed into a snarl. Have I really broken into as many pieces as the mirror? Am I whole, or broken?)

Compare your lists in groups of four. Choose the best items and combine them into a poem which begins:

'The mirror cracked.

The fragment showed me ...'

It should finish with the lines:

'The mirror cracked,

No piece of me

Was left intact.'

Compare your finished poem with another group.

3. In groups of four make a list of all the words you know which are associated with the sea (e.g. wave, sand, rocks, ship, etc.).

Then make a list of the adjectives which go with these words (e.g. rough waves, golden sand, etc.).

Then try to arrange these ideas into a 'sea poem'. Use repeated sounds if you can. It may also be helpful to include some lines which can be repeated through the poem. For example 'rolling, rolling, rolling'.

Here is an example:

▶   Rolling, rolling, rolling,
        Rough waves, ragged rocks.
        Clouds are scudding across the sky.
        Boats are bobbing on the sea.
                A storm is brewing.
        Sheltering, sheltering, sheltering,
        Silver sand and sickle shells.
                Grey gulls are flying inland,
                Heading away from the winds.
                A storm is brewing.
        Rolling, rolling, rolling,
        Rough waves, ragged rocks.
                Shivering ships are thumping through the waves.
                Sick sailors dream of watery graves
                A storm has broken.

Reading alone

Here is a poem to read on your own.

► *Reflections*

The mirror above my fireplace reflects the reflected
Room in my window; I look in the mirror at night
And see two rooms, the first where left is right
And the second, beyond the reflected window, corrected
But there I am standing back to my back. The standard
Lamp comes thrice in my mirror, twice in my window,
The fire in the mirror lies two rooms away through the window,
The fire in the window lies one room away down the terrace,
My actual room stands sandwiched between confections
Of night and lights and glass and in both directions
I can see beyond and through the reflections the street lamps
At home outdoors where my indoors rooms lie stranded,
Where a taxi perhaps will drive in through the bookcase,
Whose books are not for reading and past the fire
Which gives no warmth and pull up by my desk
At which I cannot write since I am not lefthanded.

(Louis MacNeice)

Water Picture (see p. 79)

Verses 1 and 2 – Additional words

wags:
crinkled:
dangles:
buoy:

Verses 3 and 4 – Additional words

bloom:
belly up:
sneakers:
waveringly:
swan:
hissing:
tangle:

11 The daily shuttle

Commuter

Commuter – one who spends his life
In riding to and from his wife;
A man who shaves and takes a train
And then rides back to shave again.

(E. B. White)

Warming up

🔑 1. Look at the pictures on this and the next page. Which countries were they taken in? What are the main advantages and disadvantages of each of these methods of getting to work? Make a list. Then compare it with a partner.

a)

b)

c)

d)

► 🔑 2. Listen to the recording. You will hear three different people talking about the way they get to work. Complete the grid by noting down the kind of transport they use and its advantages and disadvantages.

Person	Transport	Advantages	Disadvantages
Man 1			
Woman			
Man 2			

Compare your notes with a partner. If you do not agree, listen to the recording again.

Reading: Poem 1

1. Read this poem as you listen to the recording. Do not worry if there are things you do not understand at first.

► *The Commuters*

Well, they look like death
rocked by the early train
the commuting couple locked
together in one posture –
he, mouth open legs apart
in danger of snoring or dying;
she, hand tucked
beneath his arm, head
resting on his shoulder.   ⟫→

Sometimes at home in bed
they wake and speak
thickly with closed lids
about hanging wallpaper –
how to make it meet
over the fireplace
to keep the pattern nice and neat.
His head, rocked lower
by the swinging train,
drops till his chin
rests on her fur-bonnet;
her hands folded in a muffler
ever so prim while he
clasps his crotch
hieratically,
a Charolais King.
When those who love one another die
at first they feel nothing.
It's as if they'd had a shot
of pentathol,
as if anaesthetized.
When they feel the pain
their chief emotion is surprise
that they can feel at all.
We live so much in sleep
and habit, so close to death
in lowered consciousness,
that we scarcely notice
that we are losing breath.

(Patrick Early)

Some of the words and expressions may need explanation:

tucked: placed underneath
hanging wallpaper: sticking decorated paper on the walls of their
  home
muffler: something to keep both hands warm
crotch: between his legs
hieratically: like a priest
Charolais King: a large bull
pentathol: a kind of sleeping drug

☛ 2. Part of the poem is a description of the couple on the train. Part of it is a description of one aspect of their life at home. And another part is a commentary on people who live together for a long time. Try to mark off these three parts of the poem. Then check with a partner to see if you agree.

☛ 3. Throughout the poem, the writer is making a comparison between two things. What are they?

☛ 4. He only uses a rhyme twice in the poem. Can you find the rhymes? Why does he use them there? Compare your ideas with a partner.

Reading: Poem 2

1. Read this poem as you listen to the recording.

▶ *Fatigue*

The man in the corner
all slumped over
looks forlorner
than a tired lover,

forehead dulled
with heavy working,
eyelids lulled
by the train's jerking;

head hangs noddy,
limbs go limply,
among a number
he dozes simply;

a dumb slumber,
a dead ending,
a spent body
homeward wending.

(Peggy Bacon)

Some of the words and expressions may need explanation:

slumped: fallen in a heap, without energy
forlorner: lonelier

dulled: tired out
lulled: put to sleep
jerking: abrupt, irregular movement
noddy: moving uncontrollably back and forth in sleep
spent: exhausted
wending: travelling

2.   Try to form a mental picture of the man in the poem. How old do you think he is? What is his job? What is he wearing?

Compare your impressions with a partner.

🔑 3.   The poem has a very strongly marked rhyme scheme. Write this out using a, b, c, etc. for lines which rhyme, as in the example on p. 19. Then compare with a partner.

🔑 4.   The poem is also full of repeated sounds – both consonants and vowels. Go through the poem underlining the repeated sounds. Then check your work with a partner.

Writing

1.   Work in groups of four. Each person should write down some adjective and noun combinations which describe the weariness of commuting (e.g. tired eyes, aching feet, heavy eyelids, etc.).

The group then share all these combinations and choose the best ones. These should then be used to create a short poem about commuting. You can add other words of course to help with the rhythm or rhyme, if you wish.

Here is an example:

▶   Tired eyes,
        Aching feet,
        The commuters scramble
        For a seat.

        Each night
        They go to bed
        With heavy heart
        And sleepy head,
        Knowing tomorrow
        They must repeat,
        In weary sorrow,
        With hurrying feet,
        The tedium of today.

Compare your poem with another group.

2. Look at the picture below. Choose one of the three people in the picture and write a limerick about him. (Look again at unit 7, p. 62, to remind yourself of what a limerick is.)

Here is an example:

▶
There was a young man from Southend
Whose troubles seemed never to end.
And what with the strain
of travelling by train
He eventually went round the bend.

Compare your limerick with another group.

3. Try to write a poem for yourself about the habitual things a person does. Preferably about someone who has a very boring job.

If possible use a strong rhythm scheme. Here is an example with the strong stresses underlined:

▶
He lives in a house in the suburbs
He rises each morning at six
He runs for the bus to the station
Buys his paper and looks at the pics.

He always gets in the same carriage,
Puts his briefcase up on the rack.
Thinks miserably of his office,
And knows he can never turn back.

⠀⠀»»→

He gets to his desk by nine thirty,
Wondering what he should do.
When the coffee break comes at eleven,
He knows he still hasn't a clue.

His lunch break is quite uninspiring,
He sits it out in the canteen.
It's fish and chips, mince or potatoes,
A choice that's quite literally obscene.

At five he runs back to the station,
Gets in the same carriage again,
Unfolds his evening paper,
Pulls a veil down over his brain.

If you wish, compare your poem with a partner.

Reading alone

Here is part of a story for you to read on your own. This commuter is untypical, as he actually enjoys his journey to and from work.

▶ John Cecil lives in Essex and travels into the city every day; he's done it for thirty years; he works in a shipping insurance office.

John Cecil is a tall man with a very pink and clear skin. He has white curly hair capping his round, wide head.

And he's vigorous; he moves continually, even on the train, first lounging back in his seat and then hingeing forward, weaving from side to side before jumping to his feet to act out the part of a seagull, bus conductor or his millionaire next-door-neighbour.

He wears a dark, pinstripe suit and carries a briefcase and an umbrella; he looks like the stereotype of the London city gent yet he manages to make the daily journey into the City as individual and eventful as possible. For example, every Christmas he makes sure that his regular travelling companions bring paper hats, false noses, glasses with rotating eyes, policemen's hats, whistles which unroll when you blow them, and wine and spirits to drink. He

also persuades each person to be prepared to per-
form, to sing, to render a poem, to tell jokes or to do
special acts according to talent, like conjuring, jug-
gling and riding unicycles.

The ticket collector is always invited to join in the
party. By the time the train arrives at Cannon Street
station the ticket collector thinks that he works in the
City. He usually lurches down the platform before a
colleague seizes him from the embraces of the city
gents as they roll, helmeted and bleary eyed to their
desks to deal in gold bullion, the shares market and
international insurance.

John loves language. He revels in the precise choice
of word and in an economical and effective sentence
structure. Given that his purpose is also partly to
impress others with his general knowledge, as well as
the width of his vocabulary, his language is often
richer in imagery than the more obvious message
would seem to require.

In his work as legal adviser to a large international
shipping insurance agency he has developed his power
to be precise and unambiguous. But in working on
such barren matter his own warmth and love and
need for others and his wish to express this in words,
are dammed up. The morning and evening commuting are the only opportunities in John's day when he
can spin silvery nets of words around his neighbours.

(Andrew Wright, *John Cecil*)

12 Waking

For some people waking up in the morning is a pleasure, for others it is a torture. Some people like to get straight out of bed and meet the new day. Others prefer to burrow down deeper beneath the bedclothes and pretend that it is still night. Some look forward to the new day with hope. Others with despair.

Warming up

1. Read this passage.

> He came slowly awake with the familiar dry sensation in his mouth. His feet were as usual swollen, and he had a cramp in his neck. When would they design a plane with couchettes? A grey light was filtering through the blind over the window as they flew into the dawn. And it was cold. He eased the blanket up over his shoulders again.
>
> Down below on the grasslands, people would be

stirring in their huts, shivering in the cool of the morning. And the cattle, all leather and bone, would be making their hopeless way to the dry water-holes. And in the city his opponents would be settling to early breakfast, and talking over tactics for the coming encounter.

A ripple of images went through his mind: his wife in London, where it was midnight, asleep – safely, he hoped. And Katia snuggled with her teddy bear. The way his neighbour had been observing him during the late-night film. A sour taste came to his throat. He shifted position. His eyelids drooped. The blanket slipped again but was not replaced.

He awoke to the rustle of rearranged clothing and yawns. A plastic tray with plastic eggs and plastic bread was thrust in front of him. It was day and no going back was now possible.

(From an unpublished novel by A. Pal)

2.   Answer the following questions about yourself. (Write the answers down on a piece of paper.) Then compare your answers with a partner. Here are the questions:
— What time do you usually wake up?
— Do you usually get up straight away, or do you wait until the last moment?
— Do you dream much?
— If so do you remember your dreams? Can you remember one you have had recently?
— What do you think about when you wake up?
Keep the answers to these questions as you will need them again in the *Writing* section.

▶ ▬◗ 3.   Listen to the people on the cassette talking about waking up. Make brief notes on what each one of them says, using this grid.

Person	*Waking up/getting up time*	*Attitude to waking up/getting up*
Man 1		
Woman 1		
Man 2		
Woman 2		

Reading: Poem 1

1. Read this poem as you listen to the recording.

▶ *I'm Only Sleeping*

When I wake up early in the morning,
Lift my head, I'm still yawning.
When I'm in the middle of a dream,
Stay in bed, float up stream
(float up stream),
Please don't wake me,
no, don't shake me,
Leave me where I am, I'm only sleeping.
Everybody seems to think I'm lazy.
I don't mind, I think they're crazy
Running everywhere at such a speed,
Till they find there's no need
(there's no need),
Please don't spoil my day,
I'm miles away,
And after all, I'm only sleeping.
Keeping an eye on the world going by my window,
Taking my time, lying there and staring at the ceiling,
Waiting for a sleepy feeling.
Please don't spoil my day,
I'm miles away,
And after all I'm only sleeping.
Keeping an eye on the world going by my window,
Taking my time.
When I wake up early in the morning,
Lift my head, I'm still yawning,
When I'm in the middle of a dream,
Stay in bed, float up stream
(float up stream),
Please don't wake me,
no, don't shake me.
Leave me where I am, I'm only sleeping.

(John Lennon/Paul McCartney)

2. In groups of three discuss these expressions and try to decide what they mean:
    'float up stream'

'I'm miles away'
'Keeping an eye on'
Compare your answers with another group.

☞ 3.   Individually try to answer these questions;
– Who is the person in the poem talking to?
– He contrasts his own behaviour with other people's. Which three lines of the poem show this?

When you have finished, compare your answers with another person.

☞ 4.   In pairs make a list of all the words in the poem which have to do with *sleep* and *rest*. Compare your list with another pair.

☞ 5.   Individually mark off the parts of the poem which are repeated. There are only two sections which are not repeated. Which are these?

☞ 6.   Individually label the lines which rhyme aa, bb, etc., as in the example on p. 19. Is it a regular rhyme scheme?

When you have done this, listen to the recording again.

7.   In pairs write a summary of the poem. Use four sentences only. If you wish you may use words or phrases from the poem.

Reading: Poem 2

1.   Read this poem as you listen to the recording.

▶   *Living*

Slow bleak awakening from the morning dream
Brings me in contact with the sudden day.
I am alive – this I.
I let my fingers move along my body.
Realization warns them, and my nerves
Prepare their rapid messages and signals.
While Memory begins recording, coding,
Repeating; all the time Imagination
Mutters; You'll only die.

Here's a new day. O Pendulum move slowly!
My usual clothes are waiting on their peg.
I am alive – this I.
And in a moment Habit, like a crane,
Will bow its neck and dip its pulleyed cable,
Gathering me, my body, and our garment,

And swing me forth, oblivious of my question,
Into the daylight – why?

I think of all the others who awaken,
And wonder if they go to meet the morning
More valiantly than I;
Nor asking of this Day they will be living:
What have I done that I should be alive?
O, can I not forget that I am living?
How shall I reconcile the two conditions:
Living, and yet – to die?

Between the curtains the autumnal sunlight
With lean and yellow fingers points me out;
The clock moans: Why? Why? Why?
But suddenly, as if without a reason,
Heart, Brain and Body, and Imagination
All gather in tumultuous joy together,
Running like children down the path of morning
To fields where they can play without a quarrel:
A country I'd forgotten, but remember,
And welcome with a cry.

O cool glad pasture; living tree, tall corn,
Great cliff, or languid sloping sand, cold sea,
Waves; rivers curving: you, eternal flowers,
Give me content, while I can think of you:
Give me your living breath!
Back to your rampart, Death.

(Harold Monro)

2. With a partner check on the meanings of these words: bleak, coding, pendulum, peg, pulleyed cable, crane, oblivious, valiantly, rampant. Before you look them up in a dictionary try to work out their meaning from the context. For example, a *peg* is obviously something you put clothes on.

3. Individually make a list of all the words in the poem which have to do with *the body* (e.g. fingers). And another list of those which have to do with *the mind* (e.g. memory). Compare your lists with a partner.

4. Individually, read the poem again. As you do so, look at the following paraphrases of each verse. Choose the best paraphrase for each verse.

Waking

Verse 1 a) I wake up slowly in the morning. My body comes alive and my mind regains consciousness. In the back of my mind there is the thought that I must die.

b) As I wake up, and my mind and body pull themselves together again, I imagine that today I shall have to die.

Verse 2 a) I pray for time to slow down. Soon I shall go through my usual routine of dressing and going out. And my question 'why?' will remain unanswered.

b) I want time to move as slowly as possible. I want to know why I am alive, but force of habit will soon drive me out of the house without an answer.

Verse 3 a) I think about the other people. Perhaps they are braver than me. Maybe they don't question why they are alive. I just can't stop thinking about the fact that I have to die some day.

b) I think of other people who face the day with more courage than me. I wonder if they ask why they are alive. I just can't seem to accept that though I am alive, I shall have to die.

Verse 4 a) The sunlight touches me. The clock asks 'why?' All of a sudden I feel light-hearted. All my senses come together in harmony as I feel as if I should like to go out and play in the fields.

b) The autumn sun touches me and the clock goes on repeating my question 'why?' Quite suddenly, for no apparent reason, I feel whole again. Every part of me is filled with joy. It is a long time since I felt like this and I welcome it.

Verse 5 a) I call on all of nature to give me life. Get back inside your walls Death!

b) I think of all the wonders of nature, and pray for them to give me contentment, life and courage to resist thoughts of Death.

When you have chosen, compare your choices with a partner.

🔑 5. With a partner try to answer these three questions:
a) Which is the verse which makes a change of direction in the poem?

b) What is the question which the poet is asking in the first part of the poem?

c) Can you find another title for the poem?

Compare your answers with another pair.

🔑 6. a) Do any lines in the poem rhyme? Which ones?

b) 'Alive', 'I', 'why'. Which other words echo this sound?

Answer these questions on your own first, then compare with a partner.

🔑 7. The poem contains a number of similes and metaphors. A simile makes a comparison. For example, we say a person is 'like a toad', meaning that he is a slimy sort of person. If we had said 'He *is* a toad', this would be a metaphor. That is, in a metaphor we say that the person and the toad are one and the same. So metaphors tend to be stronger than similes. Similes are usually introduced by words or phrases such as: *like, as if . . ., as though . . ., as . . . as, seems like . . ., than . . .*, etc.

Individually try to find all the examples of metaphor or simile in the poem. There are also cases where inanimate objects are treated as if they were alive. Can you find them?

Compare your answers with a partner.

8. Individually read both poems again. Which one do you prefer? What is the main difference between them?

Discuss your answers in pairs.

Writing

1. Individually try to write a poem about 'waking'. Write WAKING vertically on the page like this:

W
A
K
I
N
G

and make each line begin with the appropriate letter. Here is an example:

Waking

▶   Waking each morning I
         Always feel the
         Killing weight of
         Indolence
         Nailing me to my
         Guilty bed.

When you have finished, work in groups of four. Compare your poems and see if you can produce a better one as a group.

2. Work in pairs. Use this framework to build up a poem about what you think of when you wake in the morning:

         I wake.
         A hundred thoughts pass through my head.
         I think of ...
         I wonder if...
         I worry about ...
         I try to remember ...
         I try to forget ...
         I hope for ...
         I pray that ...
         Reluctantly, I rise.

Compare your poem with another pair.

3. Work in pairs. Look back at the notes you made in *Warming up* 2 in answer to the questions. Look also at the notes you took when the people were talking on the recording. Try to use some of these sentences (or ideas) to make a poem like 'I'm only sleeping'. You may need only three or four key sentences or ideas. These can then be repeated in different combinations. Compare your poem with another group.

Reading alone

Here is a poem for you to read on your own.

▶ *January*

Morning: blue, cold, and still.
Eyes that have stared too long
Stare at the wedge of light
At the end of the frozen room
Where snow on a windowsill,
Packed and cold as a life,
Winters the sense of wrong
And emptiness and loss
That is my awakening.
A lifetime drains away
Down a path of frost;
My face in the looking-glass
Turns again from the light
Toward fragments of the past
That breaks with the end of sleep.
This wakening, this breath
No longer real, this deep
Darkness where we toss,
Cover a life at the last.
Sleep is too short a death.

(Weldon Kees)

13 Nobody

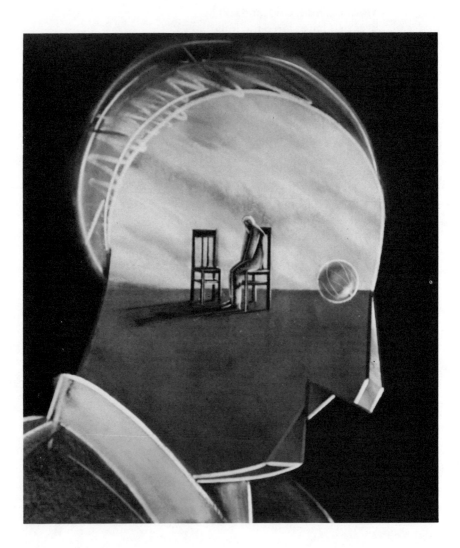

Some people feel lonely all their lives. Others only become lonely in old age. But loneliness is something which afflicts all of us at some time in our lives.

Warming up

 1. Look at this picture.

Note down the answers to these questions:
– Where is this taking place? What sort of an occasion is it?
– How would you describe the old lady's expression?
– What do you think she is thinking about?
Now compare your answers with a partner.

2. Write down ten words which you associate with the word 'lonely'.

Then compare your list with a partner and enlarge it. Finally check the entries for 'lonely' in a thesaurus/lexicon. Are they very different from your list?

3. Different groups should work simultaneously on producing lists to answer each of the following questions:

Group 1: What kinds of people feel lonely?
Group 2: What sorts of things do lonely people do/feel (e.g. cry)?
Group 3: What causes people to feel lonely?

Groups should then report back to the whole class.

▶ 🗝 4.   Listen to the recording. Various people are answering the question, 'When do you feel most lonely?'

Person	When do you feel most lonely?
Man	
Woman 1	
Woman 2	

Note down their answers individually. Then check answers in pairs.

5.   Think about your own life. Then write down a few sentences about the time you felt loneliest in your life. Choose someone else whom you would like to tell about this, and exchange experiences with him or her.

Reading: Poems 1 and 2

1.   Read these two poems as you listen to the recording.

▶   *A Sad Song About Greenwich Village*

She lives in a garret
     Up a haunted stair,
And even when she's frightened
     There's nobody to care.

She cooks so small a dinner
     She dines on the smell,
And even if she's hungry
     There's nobody to tell.

She sweeps her musty lodging
   As the dawn steals near,
And even when she's crying
   There's nobody to hear.

I haven't seen my neighbor
   Since a long time ago,
And even if she's dead
   There's nobody to know.

(Frances Park)

► *Eleanor Rigby*

Ah, look at all the lonely people.
Ah, look at all the lonely people.
Eleanor Rigby picks up the rice in the church where a wedding
   has been.
Lives in a dream.
Waits at the window, wearing the face that she keeps in a jar by
   the door,
Who is it for?
All the lonely people, where do they all come from?
All the lonely people, where do they all belong?
Father McKenzie, writing the words of a sermon that no one will
   hear,
No one comes near.
Look at him working, darning his socks in the night when there's
   nobody there.
What does he care?
All the lonely people, where do they all come from?
All the lonely people, where do they all belong?
Ah, look at all the lonely people.
Ah, look at all the lonely people.
Eleanor Rigby died in the church and was buried along with her
   name.
Nobody came.
Father McKenzie, wiping the dirt from his hands as he walks
   from the grave.
No one was saved.
All the lonely people, where do they all come from?
All the lonely people, where do they all belong?

(John Lennon/Paul McCartney)

There are a number of references which may need explanation:

rice in the church: at weddings, the guests often throw rice (or
   confetti) over the newly-married couple as they leave the church
sermon: the speech which a priest makes in church
darning: mending holes with wool
wiping the dirt from his hands: the priest usually throws a handful of
   earth onto the coffin during the burial ceremony

2.   *A Sad Song About Greenwich Village*
a) Try to work out the meaning of 'garret' from the context. Can
   you do the same with 'musty'? If not, look it up in a dictionary.
b) Choose the best paraphrase of this poem. Then check with a
   partner to see whether you agree.

   There's an old lady who lives in an attic right at the top of our
   building. She never feels really hungry so she only eats a little.

   She gets up very early to clean her room because she has
   nothing else to do. Perhaps she cries but there is no one to hear
   her. It is ages since I saw her. I wonder if she has died.

   The old lady who lives at the top of our building has no one to
   take care of her or eat with her, or sympathise with her when
   she is lonely. No one would notice if she died. Now I think of it
   – I haven't seen her for some time.

⚷   c) Notice the regularities about this poem and the structure
   of the first, third and fourth lines. Work out the rhyming scheme.
d) If you could ask the 'I' in the poem one question, what would it
   be?

3.   *Eleanor Rigby*
⚷   There are a number of problems which the poem sets us. Jot
down the answers to these problems on your own, then compare
them with a partner.
a) What makes her pick up the rice? Is it connected with her
   'dream'?
b) What is she waiting for at her window?
c) How old do you think she is?
d) 'wearing the face that she keeps in a jar by the door'. What does
   this mean?
e) Why will no one hear Father McKenzie's sermon?

f) 'buried along with her name'. What does this mean? Does it mean she was the last surviving member of her family, therefore her name died with her? Or does it mean that she had nothing else to bury with her except her name? Or does it mean both?

g) 'saved' is also ambiguous. What meanings can you give it?

4.   Which of these two poems do you prefer? Write down your reasons. Then compare notes with a partner.

Writing

1.   Look at the notes you and your partner made on the recording in *Warming up* 4. Use some of these sentences or ideas to compose a poem together. It should start with the line:

'There is no torture like loneliness.'

and finish with:

'And is there no end?'

2.   Work in pairs again. This time use the following verse structure to write a poem.

'There's nobody to ...
If/when I ...
No one to ...
.............,'

It should be written as if an old person were speaking. Here is an example:

▶   There's nobody to help me
             If I want a cup of tea,
             No one to talk to
             Except my old TV.

             There's nobody to lift me
             When I can't get out of bed.
             No one to cry on
             Or to stroke my poor old head.

             There's nobody to rely on
             When I want my shopping done,
             No one to be my friend,
             For friends I have none.

3.   Work in groups of six or seven. Each person individually

113

writes down a sentence which sums up the idea of loneliness for him or her. Every sentence is to start: 'Loneliness is ...' (e.g. Loneliness is a cold bed. Loneliness is an empty chair). The group then puts together the six or seven lines in the best order to form a poem. The group as a whole should then write a final punch line to the poem (e.g. And no end in sight).

Reading alone

Here is a poem to read by yourself.

▶ *Mrs O'Neill*

Every evening
Before she went to bed
Mrs O'Neill said
Goodnight
To the nice announcer
On her small TV
Because she was eighty
And very much alone

And when she died
He never even went
To her funeral.

(Richard Hill)

14 Pain

We all know what pain is but find it difficult to describe it or remember it objectively. Often the anticipation of pain is worse than the pain itself. And we know people react very differently to pain – some with great fortitude, others with panic.

Warming up

1. Read the following passage.

▶ Mental pain is less dramatic than physical pain, but it
is more common and also more hard to bear. The
frequent attempt to conceal mental pain increases the
burden: it is easier to say 'My tooth is aching' than to
say 'My heart is broken'. Yet if the cause is accepted
and faced, the conflict will strengthen and purify the
character and in time the pain will usually pass.
Sometimes, however, it persists and the effect is
devastating; if the cause is not faced or not recognised, it produces the dreary state of the chronic
neurotic. But some by heroism overcome even chronic mental pain. They often produce brilliant work
and strengthen, harden, and sharpen their characters
till they become like tempered steel.
[...]
Pain provides an opportunity for heroism; the opportunity is seized with surprising frequency.

(C. S. Lewis, *The Problem of Pain*)

Do you agree with what the author has to say about pain?

2. Write down five words you associate with the word 'pain'.
Then compare them with a partner and extend your list.

Finally, check on the entries under 'pain' in a thesaurus/lexicon.
How far does this correspond with your own list?

▶ ⚷ 3. Listen to the recording. On it you will hear people
talking about the most intense pain they have ever experienced.
Make notes on each speaker, then compare them with a partner.

Person	The most intense pain experienced
Woman 1	

Person	The most intense pain experienced
Man 1	
Woman 2	
Man 2	

4. Read this extract.

> ▶ Anyone who has suffered severe pain and tried to describe the experience to a friend or to the doctor often finds himself at a loss for words. Virginia Woolf, in her essay 'On Being Ill' touches on precisely this point: 'English,' she writes, 'which can express the thoughts of Hamlet and the tragedy of Lear, has no words for the shiver and the headache ... The merest schoolgirl, when she falls in love, has Shakespeare and Keats to speak for her; but let a sufferer try to describe a pain in his head to a doctor and language at once runs dry.'

The reason for this difficulty in expressing pain experiences, actually, is not because the words do not exist. As we shall soon see, there is an abundance of appropriate words. Rather, the main reason is that, fortunately, they are not words which we have occasion to use often. There is another reason: the words may seem absurd. We may use descriptors such as splitting, shooting, gnawing, wrenching or stinging, but there are no 'outside', objective references for these words. If we talk about a blue pen or a yellow pencil we can point to an object and say 'that is what I mean by yellow' or 'the colour of the pen is blue'. But what can we point to to tell another person precisely what we mean by smarting, tingling, or rasping? A person who suffers terrible pain may say that the pain is burning and add, with embarrassment (and tears) that 'it feels as if someone is shoving a red-hot poker through my toes and slowly twisting it around.' These 'as if' statements are often essential to convey the qualities of the experience.

(Ronald Melzack and Patrick Wall, *The Challenge of Pain*)

Do you agree? Discuss it with a partner.

Reading: Poems 1 and 2

1. Read these two poems as you listen to the recording.

▶   *Patient*

Praying with resignation for the skill
Of needle, draught, pill
Or for the comfort of another's touch,
For someone whom to clutch,
Though needle, draught, pill
And touch of probing hands may only kill.

Waiting with resignation for the hours
Of love, tears, flowers,
Until it is our lives we wish to spend
To gain this little end,
Though love, tears, flowers
Come only with the death of all our powers.

Listening through agonies of cold and heat
To clock, heart, feet
Moving unseen above the polished floor,
Until upon the door
There is a sudden beat
And patient and impatient surgeon meet.

(Francis King)

Some of the words may need explanation:

draught: medicine
clutch: hold tightly
probing: searching
end: result

► *Pain*

At my wits' end
And all resources gone, I lie here,
All of my body tense to the touch of fear,
And my mind,

Muffled now as if the nerves
Refused any longer to let thoughts form,
Is no longer a safe retreat, a tidy home,
No longer serves

My body's demands or shields
With fine words, as it once would daily,
My storehouse of dread. Now, slowly,
My heart, hand, whole body yield

To fear. Bed, ward, window begin
To lose their solidity. Faces no longer
Look kind or needed; yet I still fight the stronger
Terror – oblivion – the needle thrusts in.

(Elizabeth Jennings)

Some of the words may need explanation:

muffled: dulled
oblivion: total unconsciousness
thrusts: is pushed in with great power

2. *Patient*

🗝 a) Complete this paraphrase of the poem using the words at the end to fill the gaps.

The patient is lying in .... He is .... to having an .... and he .... for the necessary .... and .... Or for someone to .... him. Or to have someone to .... on to. Yet he knows that this .... might kill him.

   He looks forward to the .... time when his .... will .... with him, bring .... and so on. Yet he knows they only do this because he is ....

   He listens .... for the moment when the .... will come. Then suddenly he is there, ... to begin the ....

drugs, visiting, comfort, helpless, family, intently, sympathise, surgeon, hospital, injections, treatment, resigned, hold, operation (twice), flowers, impatient, prays

🗝 b) There are many very regular features in this poem. Look at the rhyme scheme. Look also at repetition of patterns (e.g. needle, draught, pill).

🗝 c) Can you tell who is speaking in the poem? Is it the patient?

🗝 d) There is a double meaning for the word 'patient'. Can you explain both meanings as used in 'patient and impatient surgeon'?

3. *Pain*

a) Here are two paraphrases of the poem. Choose the one you think is the better.

> I am in a panic. My body is taut with fear. Usually my mind protects me from fear by rationalising everything. But now it isn't working. Every part of me has surrendered to fear. Things look unreal and people unkind. But I'm even more afraid of the darkness of unconsciousness than of my present fear. Suddenly I feel the needle going in.

> My body has taken over control from my mind. I am paralysed

by fear. My mind can no longer provide comforting reassurance. Things and people are all hostile, threatening. I'm scared of the operation but even more of losing consciousness. I am taken by surprise as the needle goes in.

Discuss your choice with a partner. Could you improve on the paraphrase you have chosen?

🗝 b) Is there a rhyme scheme? Is it the same all through the poem?

🗝 c) Which of the two poems sounds more like 'normal' speech? Why do you think this is?

4. Which of these two poems do you prefer? And which of the two very powerful punch lines ('And patient and impatient surgeon meet', 'the needle thrusts in')? Discuss your choice with a partner.

Writing

1. Write the word PAIN vertically on a piece of paper. Then write a poem about pain using the letters for the first word of each line. For example:

> *P*atients live with it.
> *A*sthmatics breathe it.
> *I*nvalids sleep with it.
> *N*eurotics fear it.

Compare your poems in groups of four and see if you can improve the poem by using the best lines from each person.

2. With a partner look again at the notes you made on the recording in *Warming up* 3. Try to arrange some of the fragments of conversation so that they form a poem on the subject of pain. Use this as a first line if it helps you:

> 'Pain is the ambush that no one escapes.'

and this as a last line:

> 'Pain is the furnace – our bodies the fuel.'

3. Work in groups of six. Each person should remember the most painful physical experience he or she has had and write a brief sentence which conveys what it felt like.

These sentences should be discussed, and perhaps improved, by the group. Then arrange them into the best order to form a poem. The group together should decide on a good first line and last line (punch line).

4. Look back at the lists you compiled in *Warming up* 2, including the words from the lexicon.

In groups of four, use these lists to compile a poem of single words. There should be four words to a line and four lines to a verse. If possible the lines should rhyme.

Here is an example of how such a poem might begin:

> Sharp agony, aching scream,
> Throbbing, stabbing, waking dream ...

This is a kind of chant or chorus which you might like to prepare for performance for another group.

Reading alone

Here is a poem for you to read on your own.

▶   *Visiting Hour*

> The hospital smell
> combs my nostrils
> as they go bobbing along
> green and yellow corridors.
>
> What seems a corpse
> is trundled into a lift and vanishes
> heavenward.
>
> I will not feel, I will not
> feel, until
> I have to.
>
> Nurses walk lightly, swiftly,
> here and up and down and there,
> their slender waists miraculously
> carrying their burden
> of so much pain, so
> many deaths, their eyes
> still clear after
> so many farewells.

Ward 7. She lies
in a white cave of forgetfulness.
A withered hand
trembles on its stalk. Eyes move
behind eyelids too heavy
to raise. Into an arm wasted
of colour a glass fang is fixed,
not guzzling but giving.

And between her and me
distance shrinks till there is none left
but the distance of pain that neither she nor I can cross.

She smiles a little at this
black figure in her white cave
who clumsily rises
in the round swimming waves of a bell
and dizzily goes off, growing fainter,
not smaller, leaving behind only
books that will not be read
and fruitless fruits.

(Norman MacCaig)

15   Still together

'We are not the same persons this year as last; nor are those we love. It is a happy chance if we, changing, continue to love a changed person.' (W. Somerset Maugham)

Warming up

1.   Look at this picture. Write down all the words which come to mind as you look at it. Then compare your list in groups of four. Try to add items to your list.

2. Read these extracts from interviews with old people talking about their marriages.

▶ *The Valley*

We've had our ups and downs [she says]. We often look back on the old times and think, how did we do it! We don't ask for a lot now. We like our home, we like our holidays and we don't ask for much more. He can't walk much now so the other day he says 'Why don't *you* go away for a fortnight?' What, I said, and leave you? I'd be worried to death for one thing. But that's the kind of man he is. I could go out all day long and he'd see to himself. [...]

I have done the worrying for my husband. Always have done, always will. He'd say, 'Can't you leave that till tomorrow?' and I'd say, 'Tomorrow will bring its own work.' But we've always pulled together. He was really looking forward to stopping work, *really* looking forward to it. Some men don't want to retire, do they? We're better off now than we've ever been in our lives. I sometimes think of my parents who had to work so that they couldn't get old. My mother was forty-one when she died and my father fifty-five. We are advancing all the time, let's face it, we are advancing. [...]

We've had it all ways yet with all the trouble we've had we've been so happy. [...] It draws you more together when you've been through the troubles. The other day he said, 'If I had my time over again I'd still marry you.'

(Ronald Blythe, *The View in Winter*)

▶ *Prayer-Route*

My blindness has been astonishing. I remember everything about it. I remember vividly it was the 20th May and I was at a holiday home, where there were forty of us, to say morning prayers. I read the passage for the day and my sight was as clear as it had ever been. Two days later I met my wife. Three days after that I proposed to her and she accepted me. A week later, and I could not have read that same passage. I was frightened when it completely happened. It was one Saturday – we were engaged now but living apart and alone. That day I had typed six foolscap pages to friends in Canada. My fiancée rang that evening and asked how I was and I said, 'I'm fine. I've brought my correspondence right up to date – single spacing!' And we were so happy, both of us. And in that night it went, my sight. I was asleep. I noticed it when I woke. I rang my fiancée, who came immediately. [...] And from that time I have neither typed nor written nor read. I said to her, 'I'm blind. It is not the same. I'm blind. You may withdraw, you could withdraw.' But she knew then that my blindness was within God's plan for her and she said, '*Withdraw?*' From the day of my blindness I haven't felt the urge for nearly everything that absorbed me before the blindness. I go down Memory Lane and it's often better now than when it was taking place. More pleasurable. Recollections of years and years spent in God's service. It was ordered. We both felt that it was ordered. Our marriage was ordered. I think that old, widowed people should try and marry again. I think so. If they share something, some background such as we do, then they should share each other. We do. We are not just an old couple, we are deeply in love.

It would be nice if we could go out on the crest of the wave and not via the geriatric ward! To go out *good*. Pray God lets us do that, go out good.

(Ronald Blythe, *The View in Winter*)

3. Think of some old married couples you know. Are their attitudes to each other similar to or different from those expressed in the two extracts above? Make notes on the similarities or differences. Try to note down one striking incident which you have observed which illustrates their relationship especially clearly.

Then compare your notes with a partner.

Reading: Poem 1

1. Read this poem as you listen to the recording. You will be able to check on difficult words later, so do not worry about them at this stage.

▶ ## *The Old Couple*

The old couple in the brand-new bungalow,
Drugged with the milk of municipal kindness,
Fumble their way to bed. Oldness at odds
With newness, they nag each other to show
Nothing is altered, despite the strangeness
Of being divorced in sleep by twin-beds,
Side by side like the Departed, above them
The grass-green of candlewick bedspreads.

In a dead neighbourhood, where it is rare
For hooligans to shout or dogs to bark,
A footfall in the quiet air is crisper
Than home-made bread; and the budgerigar
Bats an eyelid, as sensitive to disturbance
As a distant needle is to an earthquake
In the Great Deep, then balances in sleep.
It is silence keeps the old couple awake.

Too old for loving now, but not for love,
The old couple lie, several feet apart,
Their chesty breathing like a muted duet
On wind instruments, trying to think of
Things to hang on to, such as the tinkle
That a budgerigar makes when it shifts
Its feather weight from one leg to another,
The way, on windy nights, linoleum lifts.

(F. Pratt Green)

Some words and expressions may need explanation:

bungalow: a small house with only one storey
the milk of municipal kindness: usually we speak of the milk of
   human kindness; 'municipal' refers to the local government auth-
   orities who are not generally thought of as kind, so it is ironic
fumble: move clumsily, awkwardly
at odds with: out of harmony with
nag: complain
the Departed: dead people
candlewick: a kind of cloth
budgerigar: a small bird
muted: played softly

2.   Read these two paraphrases of the poem. Which do you think is the more accurate description of the meaning? Discuss your opinion with a partner.

> The local council has given this old couple a nice new bungalow on an isolated housing estate. It is far more convenient and comfortable than their old home. There are no difficult stairs to climb, no disturbances by young people, barking dogs, etc.
>
> It is tastefully furnished. They now have twin beds to replace their old double bed. This should help them to sleep better.
>
> Overcome by the kindness of the local municipal authorities, the old couple lie contented in their beds, listening to their budgerigar.

> This old couple is struggling to come to terms with a new life, in a new bungalow provided by the local authorities. They are still as fond of each other as before. But although the new bungalow is more comfortable, it is difficult for them to get used to it. Above all, it is terribly quiet – too quiet for a couple used to living in a lively neighbourhood. They are reduced to observing each other getting older. Even the most trivial noise, like the tinkle of the budgerigar bell or the noise of the wind gives them something to measure their time by.

3.   Read *The Old Couple* again and note down all the examples of similes and metaphors. If you are unsure about the difference between simile and metaphor, look back at p. 105. For example, in line 2 'drugged' is a metaphor. The old couple were not literally drugged. Compare your list with a partner when you have finished.

Reading: Poem 2

1.   Read the poem *One Flesh* as you listen to the recording.

▶   ## One Flesh

> Lying apart now, each in a separate bed,
> He with a book, keeping the light on late,
> She like a girl dreaming of childhood,
> All men elsewhere – it is as if they wait
> Some new event: the book he holds unread,
> Her eyes fixed on the shadows overhead.

Tossed up like flotsam from a former passion,
How cool they lie. They hardly ever touch,
Or if they do it is like a confession
Of having little feeling – or too much.
Chastity faces them, a destination
For which their whole lives were a preparation.

Strangely apart, yet strangely close together,
Silence between them like a thread to hold
And not wind in. And time itself's a feather
Touching them gently. Do they know they're old,
These two who are my father and my mother
Whose fire from which I came has now grown cold?

(Elizabeth Jennings)

You may not be familiar with some of these words and expressions:

tossed up: thrown up
flotsam: pieces of wood and other rubbish which the sea throws on
   to the beach
confession: admitting something
chastity: when people do not have sexual relations
fire: in this context it means intense passion

2. Some lines in the poem raise questions. The meaning of
the poem can only be understood if we can find satisfactory answers
to these questions.
a) *One Flesh.* What is the significance of the title? (It may help to
   know that 'one flesh' is used in the Christian marriage ceremony;
   when two people marry, they become 'one flesh'.)
b) 'Lying apart now, each in a separate bed ...'. How does this
   relate to 'One Flesh'? What is the important implication of
   'now'?
c) 'it is as if they wait Some new event ...'. What new event could
   this be?
d) Why is touching each other 'like a confession Of having little
   feeling – or too much'?
e) 'Strangely apart, yet strangely close together ...'. This line seems
   to be a contradiction. Can you explain it?
     Does it have anything to do with different meanings of the
   word 'strangely'?

f) 'Silence between them like a thread to hold And not wind in ...'.
What does this mean?
 — that they are so used to each other that they do not need to
   speak?
 — that it is better not to speak in case dangerous things are
   mentioned?
 — that they have nothing left to say to each other?
 — something else?

☛ 3.   There is a strong rhyme scheme in this poem. Note it
down by using a, b, c, etc. for rhyming lines, as in the example on
p. 19. Does it form a regular pattern? Compare your notes with a
partner.

☛ 4.   As in *The Old Couple*, this poem also uses metaphors
and similes. Note down all the examples you can find. Then compare
them with a partner.

5.   Sometimes we come across 'problem lines' in poems — things
which are difficult to interpret. In this poem the expression 'All men
elsewhere' is just such a line. Discuss what it might mean in groups of
four. Compare your interpretation with another group.

☛ 6.   Both *The Old Couple* and *One Flesh* deal with the same
theme, and in each of them there are identical elements. Try to note
down the lines in each which deal with: separation; silence; growing
old; the end of physical passion. Compare your notes with a partner.

☛ 7.   What is the relationship of the poet to the couple in each
of the poems? Which poem do you prefer? Can you explain your
choice to a partner?

Writing

1.   Think back to the notes you made in *Warming up* 3 on an old
couple you are familiar with. Make a list of the things they do to pass
the time.

Then work in groups of four and share your ideas. Try to choose
eight things which old people typically do to pass the time. Then
arrange them into a group poem. Here is an example:

► He reads her the headlines
As she makes the tea,
Then they tune their set in
To Radio 3.

The washing up's something
They both do together,
Then he's off to the garden
In fair or foul weather –
While she hoovers round
Does the dusting and sings.
(It's hard to get out of the
Habit of things.)

By 11 it's time for some
Coffee and cake,
(The kind that she's only
Too happy to bake).

They're down to the pub
By opening time;
His is a pint, hers
a small gin and lime.

And so the day goes in
Small moments they share,
And old age is a pleasure,
Not something to bear.

2. Work in pairs. First of all write the word TOGETHER vertically on the page. Then try to write a poem about an old couple. Each line should begin with a word starting with the corresponding letter. Start your poem with 'Together they ...'. Here are two examples:

► Together they grow old
Only one another for company, but
Grateful for the care and tenderness
Each shows the other.
They go about their day
Hoping their lives will
End together, so neither will
Regret the other.

►
    *T*ogether they get up,
    *O*ften he makes her tea, then
    *G*oes down to light the fire.
    *E*ven on cold days
    *T*hey venture out,
    *H*e to the pub, she to the shops,
    *E*ach of them eager to
    *R*eturn together – home.

Compare your version with another pair.

3.   Imagine what your life will be like when you are 65. Make notes on:
– where you will live;
– who you will live with;
– how you will spend your day;
– what you will eat;
– what you will dislike;
– what you will like.

Compare your notes with a partner. Then try to write your own poem using your notes. It should begin like this:

    'When I'm 65
    I'll …
    I'll …'
    etc.

and end:

    'If I'm still alive, that is.'

Compare your poem with a partner. (If you prefer you can exchange notes, and use your partner's notes to write your poem.)

Reading alone

Here is another poem for you to read on your own.

▶ ### *When I'm Sixty-Four*

When I get older losing my hair
many years from now,
Will you still be sending me a Valentine
birthday greetings bottle of wine?
If I'd been out till quarter to three
would you lock the door?
Will you still need me, will you still
feed me, when I'm sixty-four?
You'll be older too
And if you say the word, I could stay with you.
I could be handy, mending a fuse
when your lights have gone.
You can knit a sweater by the fireside
Sunday morning go for a ride,
Doin' the garden, diggin' the weeds
who could ask for more.
Will you still need me, will you still feed me,
when I'm sixty-four?
Every summer we can rent a cottage,
in the Isle of Wight, if it's not too dear
we shall scrimp and save, grandchildren on your knee
Vera Chuck and Dave
send me a postcard, drop me a line,
stating point of view
indicate precisely what you mean to say
yours sincerely, wasting away
give me your answer, fill in a form
mine for evermore.
Will you still need me, will you still feed me,
when I'm sixty-four?

(John Lennon/Paul McCartney)

To the teacher

Why poetry?

This is not another anthology of the gems of English poetry, nor a handbook of literary appreciation, though it does partake a little of both. Our aim has been to make poetry accessible to students of EFL/ESL: to make it possible for them to read and enjoy it, but also to go further, and to offer them help in writing it.

The range of materials currently available to the teacher of English is wide and varied. Magazine and newspaper articles, advertisements, brochures, technical instruction manuals, business letters, and so on, are all drawn up to great effect. But poetry is all too often left to one side.

This may be because 'literature' (and especially poetry) is now considered unfashionable, or because it is thought to be too 'difficult', or irrelevant to the 'needs' of the learners.

Yet we ignore the poetic function of language at our peril. It is the cutting edge of linguistic creativity and innovation, and the key to a feel for the soul of a language. Such claims may sound dated, but the effects of a generation taught a species of EFL/ESL 'Newspeak' are there to be seen. Most of what is offered neither encourages risk-taking with the foreign language nor provides any way of approach to the poetic use of language.

In our view, there is good reason to look upon poetry simply as another variety or type of language use. Just as scientific or journalistic usage presents special kinds of problems of access, so does poetic usage. And the benefits of including poetry in our range of teaching options are considerable.

Few things are as memorable as poetry, and few memories live so long. We can often recall fragments of verse or song long after we become communicatively incompetent in a language: 'Il pleut sur la ville, comme il pleut dans mon coeur.' 'Das Kind war tot.' 'To be or not to be.' And few things can give a better instinctive sense of the rhythms and melodies of a language.

But poetry can also enhance a learner's feel for the language by giving a sense of the weight and quality of words, and the limitations of their use in everyday speech as compared with poetic writing.

If carefully selected, poems can open up themes which are common to us all whatever our cultural background, and can thus act as a powerful stimulus to the student's own reflective thinking, which will lead to more mature and fruitful group discussion.

The use of poems can also create and preserve a necessary tension between 'fluency' and 'accuracy' work. The process of discussion and arrival at consensus which characterises much of the work involved in producing a group poem, is balanced by the need to arrive at a product which is an acceptable sample of English for general consumption.

The learner can make a strong personal investment in poem-centred activities because they touch upon non-trivial areas of experience. This personal investment, combined with the interaction which necessarily follows from the group work is a powerful factor in language learning.

Finally, by encouraging learners to play with language in composing poems, in the context of support from a group, we hope to defuse their fear of it.

What is poetry?

Although it is not our intention to offer a course in poetics, it is perhaps as well to consider what is special about poetry. In other words, how do we know that one piece of language is poetry, and another is not?

Many people, if asked, would say that poetry is language which rhymes.

> 'I put my hat upon my head
> And walked into the Strand,
> And there I met another man,
> Whose hat was in his hand.'

> 'I am his Highness' dog from Kew,
> Pray tell me sir, whose dog are you?'

Yet if we asked whether the following was poetry, the answer would almost certainly be 'yes':

'The small blue flower
Dies among its petals.
The night,
And my tears,
Fall
Together.'

But this does not rhyme. So how do we know it is poetry?

The simplistic answer is 'we just know'. The slightly more technical answer is that poems make use of a variety of linguistic devices which, though they are found in 'ordinary' language, are more frequent in poetry. And in poetry they are consciously constructed to achieve an effect.

Such features include rhyme, the repetition of rhythm, the repetition of initial consonants (alliteration), inversion of grammatical patterns, the use of figurative language in the form of similes, metaphors, personification, etc., the use of semantic ellipsis, where the reader has to 'fill in' what the poet has left unsaid (as between the first and the second sentences of *The Small Blue Flower*), the use of unusual collocations, the juxtaposition of unfamiliar elements and, of course, conventions about the appearance of a poem on a page.

The effect of these and other features is to distil and heighten the meaning of the message. And this is usually achieved more economically than in prose.

Wherever it seemed appropriate or important for the understanding of the effect of a poem, we have drawn attention to these features. But, we hope, never at the expense of 'the poem itself'.

The approach

Indeed, one of the reasons that poetry provokes a shiver of awe or revulsion may be the dusty academic way in which it has so often been taught. The learner has been enmeshed in a net of iambic pentameters, sonnet rhyme schemes and classical allusions. The critical apparatus, like some unwieldy scaffolding, has obscured the clear lines of the poem constructed behind it.

If we are to use poetry in EFL/ESL contexts, then this aura of mystery has to be puffed away. Poetry must be seen both by learners and teachers as something concrete, useful and relevant.

Our choice of the poems in this book was guided by appeal and by accessibility. We first selected poems which related to common areas of human experience: love, old age, loneliness, pain, etc. We then searched for matching poems. That is, poems with the same or a related theme, thus offering students the possibility of comparing both ideas and language. This, we believe, helps increase students' awareness of stylistic variation – that there is more than one way of conveying a message, and that no one way is necessarily 'correct'.

The units do not have a uniform structure. The overall shape and length of a unit is largely determined by the poems it contains. However, certain types of activity recur throughout the book, and these are described in outline below. Moreover, every unit contains three major types of activity: framing and focussing on the theme (*Warming up*); activities to give access to the poems themselves (*Reading*); activities to promote the writing of poetry (*Writing*).

Warming up

In these activities we try to engage the students with the theme of the poems they will be reading; and particularly to get them to relate their personal experiences to it. Any of the following types of activity may be used in this section:
– listening to recorded interviews, etc., and taking detailed notes;
– brainstorming associations with the theme, e.g. colours of the days of the week, conflicts with parents, etc.;
– checking brainstorm lists against a dictionary or thesaurus;
– writing definitions of words and checking against a dictionary or thesaurus;
– comparing traditional English rhymes with those of one's own culture;
– reading brief prose extracts on the same theme and discussing them;
– reading a text on the theme; agreeing or disagreeing;
– interpreting pictures;
– drawing pictures, e.g. of early memories;
– writing out and discussing personal experiences related to the theme.

Reading: Poems

The aim here is to clear away difficulties of vocabulary and of interpretation, and to draw attention, where it is relevant, to special

features such as metre and rhyme. Any of the following activities may be used:
– giving a gloss of the meaning of culturally obscure or difficult vocabulary or expressions;
– deducing meanings from the context;
– completing a paraphrase of a poem (cloze-style);
– choosing the best paraphrase of two or three given;
– improving on a given paraphrase;
– noting the sequence of events in a poem;
– drawing attention to recurring linguistic patterns, rhyme schemes, rhythm, etc.;
– finding major similarities/differences between poems;
– framing questions to the poet or the 'I' of the poem;
– deducing the identity of the speaker in a poem;
– deducing the attitudes of the poet or 'I' in a poem;
– transformation of a poem into 'everyday' style;
– re-writing a poem to show its reverse face (e.g. *Tonight at Noon*);
– answering questions which arise from 'problem lines' in a poem;
– searching for associated groups of words;
– discussing preferences for poems.

Writing

The object here is to relieve students of some of the strain of writing by offering models, reducing the quantity to be written, and offering the support of peer discussion. Any of the following activities may be used:
– writing group poems on a given theme – one sentence per group member;
– guided writing with opening/closing lines, incomplete lines, etc.;
– using a model to imitate, e.g. limerick, parody;
– writing a theme word vertically – each line of the poem begins with a word which starts with a letter of the vertical word;
– a theme word written vertically; for each letter a word is chosen; each word must then occur somewhere in the corresponding line of the poem;
– using interview snippets to arrange into a poem;
– using interrogative/relative pronouns as the first word of each line, e.g. how, who, why, etc.;
– using mixed similes/metaphors to build a poem.

Suggestions for use

Each unit, if done thoroughly takes about three class periods. So 45 periods would be needed if you chose to use the book in its entirety. We envisage however that many teachers will prefer to use it selectively. In this case several options are open:
— only use those units which have a special appeal to the class concerned (on the basis of the theme dealt with);
— only use the *Warming up* and *Reading: Poem 1* (or 2) sections, and leave out the *Writing* section.
— select *within* each section only one or two activities. (For example, in *Running Away*: *Warming up* only do 1 and 2; *Reading: Poems 1 and 2* only do 2, 3 and 5; *Writing* only do 1 or 2.)
— set parts of each unit as work to be done outside the classroom. (For example, in *What Happened?* activities 1 and 2 in *Warming up* could be done as preparation for the classwork. In the same unit, activities 1 and 4 could be done as follow-up to the unit.)

The materials are all addressed directly to the students. We have tried in the exercises to elicit an initial response involving individual effort, followed by the support of pair or group work. We hope that this will both foster individual creativity, and bolster confidence through the sharing of difficulties. The teacher throughout has a watching brief rather than a leading role.

The units can be used in any order. The order we have chosen was one we felt comfortable with but it does not reflect a progression based on difficulty.

This is a book which has given us immense pleasure to write. We hope you will share some of our pleasure in the using of it.

Key ⚷

1 Who is today?

Warming up

1. and 3.

	Man	Why	Woman	Why
Monday	Black/grey	Colours never the same	Black	Doesn't know
Tuesday			Light blue	Sees colours as a shape on a calendar
Wednesday		Depends on mood	Yellow	which diminishes towards the middle of the week
Thursday		Has to go to work	Violet	
Friday	Purple Black	Weather not nice	Dark dark blue	
Saturday		Associates colours with feelings	White	
Sunday	Colourful – red		Red	

2 Memories

Warming up

3.

The person	Age at the time of the event	The event	Feelings about the event
Woman 1	3	Ill – flu, very bored Father improvising alphabet in cardboard Teaching her letters properly Could form words	Excited – would be able to read all books by herself
Man	5/6	Bottom of garden – large tree Making a tree house, got together bits of wood Back door with chain 'Get out' in case got caught by enemies	Lovely Exciting Enjoyable Fantastic
Woman 2	5	Lived in flats, garden at back Boy chopping up wood Walked up behind boy Axe swung back Axe went through lip Running back upstairs to Mum Towel over face Doctor came, put her to sleep at home Stitched her up in flat	Horrible Frightening

Reading: Poem 1

4.   Rhyming pattern for *Growing Pain*:

The boy was barely five years old.	a
We sent him to the little school	b
And left him there to learn the names	c
Of flowers in jam jars on the sill	d
And learn to do as he was told.	a
He seemed quite happy there until	d
Three weeks afterwards, at night,	e
The darkness whimpered in his room.	f
I went upstairs, switched on his light,	e
And found him wide awake, distraught,	g
Sheets mangled and his eiderdown	h
Untidy carpet on the floor.	i
I said 'Why can't you sleep? A pain?'	j
He snuffled, gave a little moan,	k
And then he spoke a single word:	l
'Jessica.' The sound was blurred.	l
'Jessica? What do you mean?'	m
'A girl at school called Jessica,	n
She hurts –' he touched himself between	m
The heart and stomach '– she has been	m
Aching here and I can see her.'	o
Nothing I had read or heard	l
Instructed me in what to do.	p
I covered him and stroked his head.	q
'The pain will go, in time'. I said.	q

This is not a regular rhyming pattern.

Reading: Poem 2

2.   My __father__ says that when I was very young, I came __downstairs__ in the early __hours__ of the morning. I was obviously still __half-asleep__. Anyway, I sat down in __front of__ the fire, my __dummy__ in my mouth, and just __stared__ into the __fire__. My father had been up late __working__. He asked __what__ had woken me up. And my __reply__, which he remembers to this day was, 'A wolf __dreamed__ me.'

3 Running away

Warming up

2.

Person	What did you and your parents disagree about?
Woman 1	Almost everything Didn't want to study anything that would lead to a specific career
Man 1	Friends Values he held Hair and dress
Woman 2	Staying out late without letting them know where she was Make up Reading comics e.g. Valentine
Man 2	Homework Career - he wanted to be an actor; parents wanted him to go to university and take a degree in forestry

Reading: Poems 1 and 2

2. *What Has Happened to Lulu?*
First, Lulu took her money-box. Then she climbed through the window, after leaving a note for her mother. There were voices and the sound of an engine as Lulu left (perhaps someone collected her). There may have been an argument between Lulu and her mother, because a cry of anger or pain was heard. Or perhaps Lulu's mother cried out when she found Lulu's note.

The order of events is not made clear in the poem.

She's Leaving Home
At 5 am on a Wednesday, a young girl got out of bed very quietly so as not to wake her parents. She left a note and then crept downstairs to the kitchen. She opened the back door very quietly and left the house.

Her mother woke up, while her father was still asleep, put on her dressing-gown and found the note her daughter had left. The mother began to cry after she had read the note and woke her husband. She explained that their daughter had left home.

By Friday morning, the girl was already a long way from home. She had arranged a meeting with a man she knew, who had a job connected with cars.

3. Both girls leave home.
   Both girls leave during the night.
   Both leave a note.
   Both mothers cry.
   Both girls meet someone with whom they run away (probably).

4. *What Has Happened to Lulu?*
   The speaker is probably Lulu's younger sister or brother. The father is not mentioned in the poem (perhaps there isn't a father?) and the mother refuses to tell the speaker anything about what has happened to Lulu.
   She's Leaving Home
   There are different speakers in the poem: someone describing the girl's departure, the mother and also probably the father. The father seems much less involved and less upset by his daughter running away. There has obviously been very little communication between parents and daughter.

5. *What Has Happened to Lulu?*
   The mother is sad and possibly angry. She is at a loss as to what to do and tries to shield the younger sister/brother from knowledge.
   She's Leaving Home
   The words 'our baby' and 'Daddy' are revealing. 'our *baby*' shows that the mother still treated her teenage daughter as a baby rather than letting her grow up. The mother believes that her daughter has been selfish, thinking only of herself and not her parents who, according to the mother, sacrificed their lives for their daughter. 'Daddy' shows that the mother saw her husband as her daughter's 'daddy', and the relationship between them as husband and wife may not have been satisfactory.

6. a) Why are you turning your head, mother?
   Why are you crying?
   Why have you crumpled up the note and put it on the fire?
   Why are you pretending that you haven't put anything on the fire?
   Why did you tell me that I must have dreamt the noises which I heard last night?
   Why are you wandering about as if you don't know what to do?

b) The old rag-doll and the money-box are clues about Lulu's age (probably in her mid-teens).

7. a) The note probably said:
   'Mum and Dad,
   I have to leave. I can't live with you any more. I have to get away. Don't worry. I'll be all right.'
   She might also have said:
   'I know you think you have given me everything you could. You did give me a lot. But they were always material things – things which could be bought. What I needed most – love, companionship, warmth, laughter and fun – you never gave me.'
   b) It implies that she has been/is crying and shows that she is very sad to be leaving home in some ways, and that it was a difficult decision.
   c) It means that there has been so little meaningful communication between daughter and parents, so little love and warmth, that she has been living alone in effect.
   d) It tells us that the mother still thinks of her daughter as a small child, ignoring the fact that she has grown up and has a personality and needs of her own.
   e) It shows that she thinks she has been solely responsible for their daughter, that she thinks of herself first, forgetting about her husband and what he may feel.
   f) It is unlikely to be true. They did not understand their daughter at all, so although they may have thought they were doing their best for her, it was all irrelevant.
   g) The mother doesn't understand that they could have failed their daughter. They gave her everything money could buy, and she doesn't understand that the daughter needed all the things money couldn't buy as well.
   h) Fun, love, warmth and close friendship were all missing within the family.
   i) She travelled to the place where her appointment would be – quite a distance away.

4 Goodbyes

Reading: Poem 1

3. A man is speaking to the woman he loves.
4. This is a regular rhyming scheme. The second and fourth lines rhyme in each verse.

Goodbye

So we must say Goodbye, my darling,   *a*
And go, as lovers go, for ever;   *b*
Tonight remains, to pack and fix on labels   *c*
And make an end of lying down together.   *b*

I put a final shilling in the gas,   *d*
And watch you slip your dress below your knees *e*
And lie so still I hear your rustling comb   *f*
Modulate the autumn in the trees.   *e*

And all the countless things I shall remember   *g*
Lay mummy-cloths of silence round my head;   *h*
I fill the carafe with a drink of water;   *i*
You say 'We paid a guinea for this bed,'   *h*

And then, 'We'll leave some gas, a little warmth *j*
For the next resident, and these dry flowers,'   *k*
And turn your face away, afraid to speak   *l*
The big word, that Eternity is ours.   *k*

Your kisses close my eyes and yet you stare   *m*
As though God struck a child with nameless fears; *n*
Perhaps the water glitters and discloses   *o*
Time's chalice and its limpid useless tears.   *n*

Everything we renounce except our selves;   *p*
Selfishness is the last of all to go;   *q*
Our sighs are exhalations of the earth,   *r*
Our footprints leave a track across the snow.   *q*

We made the universe to be our home,   *s*
Our nostrils took the wind to be our breath,   *t*
Our hearts are massive towers of delight,   *u*
We stride across the seven seas of death.   *t*

Yet when all's done you'll keep the emerald   *v*
I placed upon your finger in the street;   *w*
And I will keep the patches that you sewed   *x*
On my old battledress tonight, my sweet.   *w*

Reading: Poem 2

4. Rhyming scheme:

At Parting

Since we through war awhile must part	a
Sweetheart, and learn to lose	b
Daily use	c
Of all that satisfied our heart:	a
Lay up those secrets and those powers	d
Wherewith you pleased and cherished me these two years.	e
Now we must draw, as plants would,	f
On tubers stored in a better season,	g
Our honey and heaven;	h
Only our love can store such food.	i
Is this to make a god of absence?	j
A new-born monster to steal our sustenance?	k
We cannot quite cast out lack and pain.	l
Let him remain – what he may devour	m
We can well spare:	n
He never can tap this, the true vein.	l
I have no words to tell you what you were,	o
But when you are sad, think, Heaven could give no more.	p

Words which almost rhyme:
Verse 1: lose–use
        powers–years
Verse 2: would–food
        season–heaven
        absence–sustenance
Verse 3: devour–spare
        were–more

5 What happened?

Warming up

4.

Person	What happened?
Woman 1	Fell in love with unsuitable people Met a man – he told her he was in love with someone else Went to 'ladies' Now wishes she'd thrown teapot at him
Woman 2	Often had relationships because scared of being on own Theatre director – he was very boring, though did useful things When broke up she felt free – great relief
Man	Fell in love at 15/16 with girl – very beautiful Used to sketch her Cycled long way round to see her Plucked up courage to invite her to a dance – tongue-tied She left town with parents; he was desolate Returned one year later He saw that she was spotty, pale, overweight

Reading: Poems 1 and 2

2. d) The first six lines of the poem are repeated at the end. Also, 'I'm looking through you, (you're not the same)' and 'I'm looking through you (and you're nowhere)' are repeated, each followed by 'Why, tell me why did you not treat me right? Love has a nasty habit of disappearing overnight'.

3. a) a simile – This is an expression or phrase which makes a comparison to help describe something. Similes are usually introduced by words or phrases such as: *like, as, as if ..., as though ...*, etc. For example, in the poem, 'soft *as* an open mouth' is used to describe the softness of the girl's lips.

outside common usage – Using a word or expression in a way which is not normally understood or accepted in everyday language.

implying – Stating something indirectly; suggesting.

a black eye – The expression used to describe the colour of the skin around the eye when you have received a blow to the eye, usually in a fight.

answering to such a description – We know of no one who fits the picture you have given us of that person.

b) Features of poem: – layout on page;
- use of repeated sounds, e.g. 'Her *h*air *h*ung *h*eavily';
- unusual use of language, e.g. policemen don't usually ask for similes.

6 It's mine...

Reading: Poem 1

2. 'my linen heart'
'these rigid, lumpy arms'
'these blue eye-smudges'
'this sewn-up mouth'

Reading: Poem 2

2. a) The boy at the window
b) The boy at the window
c) The boy at the window
d) The snowman

4. Despite what the boy thinks, the snowman is quite happy to be outside because he doesn't want to go inside and melt. Even so, the snowman is touched by the boy's tears. The snowman is made of ice, but he melts a little so that it seems as if a tear drop is running from his eye. He is moved at the sight of the boy at the window, who is in such a warm, light, loving home, yet is so frightened.

5. Rhyming scheme:

Boy at the Window

Seeing the snowman standing all alone	*a*
In dusk and cold is more than he can bear.	*b*
The small boy weeps to hear the wind prepare	*b*
A night of gnashings and enormous moan.	*a*
His tearful sight can hardly reach to where	*b*
The pale-faced figure with bitumen eyes	*c*
Returns him such a god-forsaken stare	*b*
As outcast Adam gave to Paradise.	*c*
The man of snow is, nonetheless, content,	*d*
Having no wish to go inside and die.	*e*
Still, he is moved to see the youngster cry.	*e*
Though frozen water is his element,	*d*
He melts enough to drop from one soft eye	*e*
A trickle of the purest rain, a tear	*f*
For the child at the bright pane surrounded by	*e*
Such warmth, such light, such love, and so much fear.	*f*

The pattern is regular. (Note that sometimes poets use weak rhymes to complete a pattern, e.g. 'eyes', 'Paradise'.)

7 Nonsense!

Warming up

2. Rhymes like this appeal to children because of their strong rhythm. They often form the basis of children's playground games. The children chant the rhyme while skipping or jumping. The nonsensical nature of the rhyme appeals to children's humour.

Reading: Poems 1 and 2

2. b) Today at noon
   Supermarkets will advertise 3d off everything
   Today at noon
   Children from unhappy families will be sent to live in a home
   Humans will tell each other elephant jokes
   America will declare war on Russia

*In remembrance of the dead of World War I, poppies will be sold in
    the streets on November 11th
The first colours of autumn will appear
When the leaves fall from the trees

Today at noon
Cats will hunt pigeons through city backyards
Churchill will tell us to fight on the beaches and on the landing fields
A tunnel will be built under the river at Liverpool
*Planes will be sighted flying in formation over Woolton
*and Nelson has not only lost his eye but his arm as well
  Black Americans will demonstrate for equal rights in front of the
    White House
and Dr Frankenstein has just created the Monster

Girls in bikinis are sunbathing
*Folksongs are being sung by extraordinary people
Art galleries are open to everyone
Pop singers get their songs in the Top 20
Politicians are elected to Parliament
There are jobs for no one and everyone wants them
In back alleys everywhere teenage lovers are kissing in the dark
In forgotten graveyards everywhere the living will quietly bury the
    dead
And
*You will never tell me you love me
Today at noon

* = problem lines

3. a) As things are at present, people don't touch or talk to each other
easily. They do not readily show feelings of love and warmth towards
one another. People these days are often confused, tied up in their
own personal problems. Today, work is complicated and often
drawn out. Leisure time is planned and is sometimes loud and
boisterous. People are always in a rush, watching the clock. Today
people need a reason to smile.

4. In both poems, the poets create a reversal of aspects of life. The major
difference, however, is that one appears to be nonsense and is pessimis-
tic, whereas the other appears to be more possible and is optimistic.

8 Construction

Warming up

2.

Person	Feelings about new construction
Man 1	Thinks about old buildings not new buildings Believes we destroyed many beautiful old buildings in 60s and 70s which we can't replace We have built up-ended tissue boxes There are few new buildings we can admire Why don't we keep old buildings?
Woman 1	Has feelings of horror and sadness, also smugness – won't have to live there New buildings are soulless, destroy character of the area Hates new construction
Woman 2	Excited by new buildings, full of anticipation; interesting new buildings There's a lot of new building round where she lives because bombed in war – some of buildings are wonderful, mirror sky and trees – beautiful One building – white, cross between wedding cake and space ship, beautiful Might write note to architect saying how lovely it is
Man 2	Depends on building Houses – filled with hope Money being put into building and lots of jobs for builders Very optimistic

Reading: Poems 1 and 2

2. a) The _____writer_____ is standing with the _____woman_____ he _____loves_____, looking out of the window of his own _____apartment_____ at the _____construction_____ site _____opposite_____. He imagines the _____cranes_____ are drawing _____pictures_____ in the _____air_____ of the _____apartments_____ which will later be _____built_____ there. He goes on to _____ask_____ whether the ghosts of the _____people_____ who will _____live_____ opposite are _____looking_____ at them, and whether their _____hearts_____ will be as much _____in tune_____ as his with his lover's.

4. Both poems are about construction and construction sites. The speakers in each poem are people in love. They use the images of the shape and strength of the buildings as points against which they can measure their love.

9   The takeover

Reading: Poems 1 and 2

2. a) discreetly
     very quietly
     soft
     voiceless
     bland-mannered
     asking little or nothing
     meek

   b) take hold
     acquire
     make room
     fists insist on
     heaving
     hammers
     rams
     widen
     shoulder
     nudgers
     shovers
     multiplies
     foot

4. Fungi/insects taking over the earth.
   Both require little to survive: mushrooms – water;
                                     flies – waste matter.
   Both are small creatures, coming in large numbers.

10 On reflection

Warming up

1.

a) Amsterdam, Holland

c) Kashmir, India

b) Mandalay, Burma

d) Shoreham, Sussex, England

Reading: Poem 1

3. flag – fishhook
   arched stone bridge – eye
   pink balloon – buoy
   cherry bloom – roots
   a hill – glass bowl
   a swan – the figure three
   the bridge – a fan

4. chimneys bouncing
   a flag wags
   birds coast
   a swan kisses
   water-windows splinter
   tree-limbs tangle
   the bridge folds

5. pond   park
   in (2)   things   buildings   wriggle   chimneys
   bent   legs
   bent   bouncing   below
   bouncing   clouds
   flag   wags
   flag   fishhook
   bridge   is   underlid   in (2)   its   dip   crinkled   with
   heads   hats
   barking   backs   baby
   baby   taken
   ducks   dangle   down
   balloon   buoy
   bloom   birds   belly-up
   buoy   deploy
   bloom   roots
   bowl   bottom   bunch
   bunch   peanut   munching   suspended
   suspended   sneakers
   forming   figure
   swan   steers
   two   towers
   three   between
   dimpled   doubled
   hissing   kisses   herself   scene   splinter
   hissing   kisses   splinter   limbs   bridge

>>>→

water   windows
tree   tangle
folds   fan

(Students will probably find several other examples not included in this list.)

Reading: Poem 2

2. Verse 1   anchored – firmly fixed (usually of boats and ships)
             swirled – twisted (of liquid)
   Verse 2   fathoms – depths (of water)
             seaweed – plants growing in the sea
   Verse 3   shallows – water which is not very deep
             wading – walking up to one's knees or thighs in water
   Verse 4   gulls – sea birds
             a ripple – a small wave on the water

3. *Words associated with the sea:*
   anchored drowning swirled bay lighthouse moored fathoms
   seaweed boat floated underwater shallows wading sand
   harbour drowned gulls net ripple swam sea drowned

Adjective/noun combinations:	*Usual combination:*
drowning bells	drowning people
underwater wind	underwater current
red-roofed shallows	red-roofed houses
clouded sand	clouded sky
knee-deep harbour	knee-deep water

4. – In the water below me, I could see a reflection of the sky and what appeared to be a boat floating upside down.
   – I could see a reflection of the sky and seagulls in the water. When I looked in the reflection, it seemed as if the birds were falling from the sky into the water.
   – As the sky could be seen reflected in the water, it looked as if the ripples of water were moving across the sky.
   – When I looked at the reflection of my arm in the water and then moved my arm towards me, it looked as if it was moving up through the water to meet me with a swimming action.

5. There is a pattern. In each verse, lines 1, 4 and 6 end with a similar sound, but this is generally not strong enough to be called a rhyme, except for 'town' 'down' in the first verse, and 'death' 'breath' in the last verse. Lines 5 and 6 in the fourth verse almost rhyme.

Repeated sounds:
tower   crowned   town
tower   town
houses   round   drowning   down
round   rolled
bells   bubbles
burned   bay
moored   mirroring
seaweed   swayed
boat   below
boat   floated
underwater   wind
ruffled   red-roofed
where   wading
stilt-legged   stood
down   deep   drowned
down   drowned
ladder   led
gulls   fell
net   met
met   image
window   water
slurred   sky   swam
hand   swam
meet   me   met   myself
underworld   water
saw   sway
face   sway
day   underneath
spoke   speaking
spoke   moment   broke
broke   breath

6. In *Water Picture* the picture shatters when the swan disturbs the water by dipping its beak in it: 'Fondly hissing ... folds like a fan.' In *The Waterglass* the picture shatters when the speaker disturbs his image in the water by speaking: 'I spoke to my speaking likeness, and the moment broke with my breath.'

11 The daily shuttle

Warming up

1. a) Paris, France
    b) Bangkok, Thailand
    c) Calcutta, India
    d) Holland

2.

Person	Transport	Advantages	Disadvantages
Man 1	Motorbike	Wakes you up Can't be asleep Quick Cheap Efficient Enjoyable	
Woman	Car Tube	Quick	Tedious Have to change Exhausting
Man 2	Tube	Very quick Convenient Best way to travel	

Reading: Poem 1

2. Description of the couple on the
   train: 'Well, they look like death'
    to 'Resting on his shoulder'
  and 'His head, rocked lower'
    to 'A Charolais King.'
Description of one aspect of their life
  at home: 'Sometimes at home in bed'
    to 'to keep the pattern nice and neat.'
A commentary on people who live together for a
  long time: 'When those who love one another die'
    to 'that we are losing breath.'

3. The poet likens the way in which people lead their lives with dying and death, 'We live so much in sleep and habit, so close to death ...'.

4. 'meet' and 'neat' form a pattern in the poem, just as matching the two pieces of wallpaper forms the pattern in the wallpaper design. The rhyme emphasises the image of a neat and tidy pattern, and the couple's concern with trivial details.

   'death' and 'breath' also rhyme, which is important as they are at the end of the poem, as at the end of life. The rhyme here emphasises the whole significance of the poem.

Reading: Poem 2

3. Rhyming scheme:

Fatigue

The man in the corner	a
all slumped over	b
looks forlorner	a
than a tired lover,	b
forehead dulled	c
with heavy working,	d
eyelids lulled	c
by the train's jerking;	d
head hangs noddy,	e
limbs go limply,	f
among a number	g
he dozes simply;	f
a dumb slumber,	g
a dead ending,	h
a spent body	e
homeward wending.	h

In the first verse, 'over' and 'lover' have different vowel sounds, of course, but this is acceptable as a (weak) rhyme in English poetry.

4. Repeated sounds:
   looks forlorner lover
   forehead heavy
   eyelids lulled
   head hangs
   limbs limply
   among number
   dumb slumber
   dumb dead ending
   ending spent wending
   homeward wending

12 Waking

Warming up

3.

Person	Waking up/getting up time	Attitude to waking up/getting up
Man 1	2 pm	His metabolism doesn't function until then Hates getting up in the morning especially in winter, but has to because of work
Woman 1	Must get up within 5 minutes of alarm going off	Quite good about getting up Can't talk in the morning Her dream – to have a white-coated waiter quietly bringing in croissants, coffee, orange juice
Man 2	No specific time except early when on holiday	He says it's an attitude of mind His metabolism doesn't get going early except on holiday e.g. when he was in Indonesia he could get up early whether light or dark It has to do with what's on that day partly

Person	*Waking up/getting up time*	*Attitude to waking up/getting up*
Woman 2	No specific time, except early when on location	She doesn't really like getting up early But if she has to go on location early, she gets a feeling of self-satisfaction of being the only one creeping around the house while others sleep – she thinks this self-satisfaction shows a nasty side to her character

Reading: Poem 1

2. Float up stream: The current of a river carries things with it – down stream. The idea here is that the world is going about its business in one direction, and the dreamer is going in another, *against* the current.

I'm miles away: The dream which the person is having in the poem seems to carry him miles away from the events of real life.

Keeping an eye on: While the person in the poem is waiting for sleep to come, he is watching events/people going by his window.

3. The speaker could be talking to his parents or anybody else who lives in the same house – asking them not to wake him.

He contrasts his own behaviour with other people's: 'Everybody seems to think I'm lazy. I don't mind, I think they're crazy Running everywhere at such a speed.'

4. yawning   dream   bed   sleeping   lying   sleepy

5. Parts of the poem which are repeated:
   'When I wake up ... I'm only sleeping'   (×2)
   'Please don't spoil my day ... taking my time'   (×2)
   Parts which are not repeated:
   'Everybody seems to think ... (there's no need)'
   'lying there ... sleepy feeling'

6. Rhyming scheme:

I'm Only Sleeping

When I wake up early in the morning,	a
Lift my head, I'm still yawning.	a
When I'm in the middle of a dream,	b
Stay in bed, float up stream	b
(float up stream),	b
Please don't wake me,	c
no, don't shake me,	c
Leave me where I am, I'm only sleeping.	d
Everybody seems to think I'm lazy.	e
I don't mind, I think they're crazy	e
Running everywhere at such a speed,	f
Till they find there's no need	f
(there's no need),	f
Please don't spoil my day,	g
I'm miles away,	g
And after all, I'm only sleeping.	d
Keeping an eye on the world going by my window,	h
Taking my time, lying there and staring at the ceiling,	i
Waiting for a sleepy feeling.	i
Please don't spoil my day,	g
I'm miles away,	g
And after all I'm only sleeping.	d
Keeping an eye on the world going by my window,	h
Taking my time.	j
When I wake up early in the morning,	a
Lift my head, I'm still yawning,	a
When I'm in the middle of a dream,	b
Stay in bed, float up stream	b
(float up stream),	b
Please don't wake me,	c
no, don't shake me,	c
Leave me where I am, I'm only sleeping.	d

The first two eight-line sections and the last eight-line section of the poem follow a regular pattern.

Reading: Poem 2

3. Words which have to do with the body:
   fingers   body   nerves   neck   Heart   Brain
   Words which have to do with the mind:
   Memory   Imagination

5. a) Verse 4
   b) Why do I have to die?

6. a) The last lines of each of the first four verses rhyme, and 'breath' and 'Death' in the last verse.
   b) cry   die

7. Metaphors: 'my nerves Prepare their rapid messages and signals'
               'While Memory begins recording, coding, Repeating'
               'Imagination Mutters'
               'My usual clothes are waiting on their peg'
               'Habit, ... Will bow its neck and dip its pulleyed cable Gathering me, my body and our garment, And swing me forth, oblivious of my question'
               'the autumnal sunlight With lean and yellow fingers points me out'
               'The clock moans'
               'the path of morning'
   Similes: 'Habit, *like* a crane, Will bow its neck'
             'Heart, Brain and Body, and Imagination All gather in tumultuous joy together, Running *like* children down the path of morning'
   Inanimate objects treated as if they were alive: clothes
                                            sunlight
                                            clock

13   Nobody

Warming up

1. The fact that the old lady is wearing a paper hat suggests that she is at some sort of party—perhaps it is Christmas in an old people's home. She looks sad—perhaps she is thinking about Christmasses in the past.

4.

Person	When do you feel most lonely?
Man	When he is in a crowd, for example, in Woolworth's or in a crowd in the street
Woman 1	In an audience, for example, in a cinema when everyone laughs at something which she personally finds upsetting or moving
Woman 2	When she goes back to her flat after she has been away for a few days – everything is neat and tidy but the flat feels empty and makes her feel empty and lonely

Reading: Poems 1 and 2

2. c) Rhyming scheme:

A Sad Song About Greenwich Village

She lives in a garret	a
Up a haunted stair,	b
And even when she's frightened	c
There's nobody to care.	b
She cooks so small a dinner	d
She dines on the smell,	e
And even if she's hungry	f
There's nobody to tell.	e

She sweeps her musty lodging	g
As the dawn steals near,	h
And even when she's crying	i
There's nobody to hear.	h
I haven't seen my neighbor	j
Since a long time ago,	k
And even if she's dead	L
There's nobody to know.	k

First line regularities in first three verses: She lives, She cooks, She sweeps ...
Third line regularities in all four verses: And even when/if ...
Fourth line regularities in all four verses: There's nobody to ...

3. a) Eleanor Rigby is dreaming of getting married herself, or possibly she wasn't invited to the wedding but dreamt that she had been. She picked up the rice and pretended that she had been one of the people throwing it.
   b) She is hoping someone, perhaps a lover, will come.
   c) Open question.
   d) Eleanor Rigby is wearing make up on her face. She keeps this in a jar near the door.
   e) Because nobody in the village or town goes to church.
   f) It probably means both. In addition to the two interpretations given, it could mean that nobody will remember her either as a person they had seen in the village or town, or by her name. She was insignificant and went unnoticed.
   g) – No one can be saved from death.
      – The person being buried cannot be 'saved', i.e. kept in memory, remembered.
      – It also has a religious meaning: no one would go to heaven, no one's soul would be saved.

14   Pain

Warming up

3.

Person	The most intense pain experienced
Woman 1	Finds it hard to remember physical pain – brain blocks it out She spent a long time in hospital at age of 14 - but has no memory of pain Remembers emotional pain more Her father died 18 months ago - created a physical pain in stomach/chest like a big hole – kept rubbing it to make it go away
Man 1	Agrees that emotional pain comes to mind more easily Recently dislocated shoulder playing judo – felt helpless, sick Says that one tries to relax but when pain is great it overwhelms one His coach reassured him, but, if alone, it would have been hard to stop pain engulfing him
Woman 2	Able to shut off minor pain and believes that mind blanks out serious physical pain She can remember having a migraine Pain was all enveloping – it took over her body and mind and her mind couldn't help her get out of it She found that pain terrifying – it was accompanied by nausea, spots before the eyes, agony in the brain She was unable to shut out the light even under the bed covers
Man 2	The most intense pain he remembers was a dentist removing a tooth - the tooth broke and the dentist had to dig into the gum to get it out This took place on a Friday, so he was in intense pain on Saturday and Sunday when he couldn't see dentist Can only remember the incident, not the actual pain

Reading: Poems 1 and 2

2. a) The patient is lying in _hospital_. He is _resigned_ to having an _operation_ and he _prays_ for the necessary _drugs_ and _injections_. Or for someone to _comfort_ him. Or to have someone to _hold_ on to. Yet he knows that this _treatment_ might kill him.

   He looks forward to the _visiting_ time when his _family_ will _sympathise_ with him, bring _flowers_ and so on. Yet he knows they only do this because he is _helpless_. He listens _intently_ for the moment when the _surgeon_ will come. Then suddenly he is there, _impatient_ to begin the _operation_.

   b) Rhyming scheme:

Patient

Praying with resignation for the skill	a
Of needle, draught, pill	a
Or for the comfort of another's touch,	b
For someone whom to clutch,	b
Though needle, draught, pill	a
And touch of probing hands may only kill.	a
Waiting with resignation for the hours	c
Of love, tears, flowers,	c
Until it is our lives we wish to spend	d
To gain this little end,	d
Though love, tears, flowers	c
Come only with the death of all our powers.	c
Listening through agonies of cold and heat	e
To clock, heart, feet	e
Moving unseen above the polished floor,	f
Until upon the door	f
There is a sudden beat	e
And patient and impatient surgeon meet.	e

Repetition of patterns:

'Of needle, draught, pill'	Verse 1 line 2
'Though needle, draught, pill'	Verse 1 line 5

'Of love, tears, flowers'   Verse 2 line 2
'Though love, tears, flowers'   Verse 2 line 5

'To clock, heart, feet'   Verse 3 line 2
'There is a sudden beat'   Verse 3 line 5
(There is a connection here because we talk about clocks and hearts beating.)

   c) The speaker could possibly be the patient. However, it could equally be someone who has been a patient before or someone who is a relative of the patient.
   d) 'Patient' is both the person in hospital and the adjective connected with 'patience'.

3. b) Lines 1 and 4, and 2 and 3 form a pattern. The poet has sometimes used weak rhymes in the pattern and sometimes stronger ones.
      In verse 1 'here' 'fear' is a strong rhyme and there is a partial rhyme of 'end' and 'mind'. In verse 2 'nerves' 'serves' is a strong rhyme and there is a partial rhyme of 'form' and 'home'. In verse 3, however, there are only two partial rhymes: 'shields' and 'yield' and 'daily' and 'slowly'. In verse 4, lines 1 and 4, and 2 and 3 rhyme.
   c) *Pain* sounds more like 'normal' speech because the lines flow smoothly into each other and the rhymes and rhythm are not as obvious and strong as in *Patient*.

15   Still together

Reading: Poem 1

3. Metaphors: '*Drugged* with the milk of municipal kindness'
               '*divorced* in sleep by twin-beds'
   Similes: 'Side by side *like* the Departed'
            'A footfall in the quiet air is crisper *than* home-made bread'
            '*as* sensitive to disturbance *as* a distant needle is to an earthquake'
            'Their chesty breathing *like* a muted duet on wind instruments'

Reading: Poem 2

2. a) The title can be interpreted in several ways. For example, the couple met many years ago, fell in love, married and became, as the Christian marriage ceremony states, one flesh; that is, united in mind and body.

A different meaning is suggested, however, by the events in the poem connected with the usual meaning of the word flesh. Flesh usually refers to the human body as distinct from the mind, soul or spirit. In the poem, we read about two bodies (or flesh) from which the original life, love and passion have disappeared. In this sense, the title *One Flesh* creates a morbid picture of two people whose lives are spent and who approach death.

b) When the couple were first married, they presumably slept in one bed, consummated their marriage and had children, hence 'one flesh', meaning 'united in body'. But now they are old and sleep in separate beds. 'Now' implies that *before* they did not lie apart.

c) The new event could be death.

d) When the old couple do remember to touch each other, i.e. show affection, they feel guilty at not having done so more often. Or the old couple may think that they should no longer need to touch one another, as if with age passion is wrong and therefore they feel guilty.

e) The couple are apart in the sense that they sleep in separate beds and their minds wander off on their own trains of thought. They no longer make love or show love for one another in an overt way. Yet, they *are* together in that they share so much of the past and both their lives are going in the same direction. They are both waiting for death to approach.

'Strangely' carries the meaning 'oddly'. This matches the oddness or contradictoriness of the line 'Strangely apart, yet strangely close together'.

f) Whereas normally another person's voice would be a reminder of that person's presence, the old couple hold on to the familiar *silence* between them as a reminder of each other's existence. They have no need to talk to one another and perhaps it is better not to mention certain things.

3. The rhyming scheme is not totally regular. In the first two verses lines 2 and 4 rhyme and the other lines either have a strong rhyme, e.g. 'bed', 'unread', 'overhead', or a partial rhyme, e.g. 'passion', 'destination'. In the last verse alternate lines rhyme, although 'mother' is only a weak rhyme with 'feather' and 'together'.

4. Metaphors: 'And *time itself's a feather* touching them gently'
   'Whose *fire* from which I came has now grown cold'
   Similes: 'She *like* a girl'
   'Tossed up *like* flotsam from a former passion'
   'They hardly ever touch, or if they do it is *like* a confession'
   'Silence between them *like* a thread to hold'

6.	*The Old Couple*	*One Flesh*
Separation:	'divorced in sleep by twin-beds' 'The old couple lie, several feet apart'	'Lying apart now, each in a separate bed'
Silence:	'In a dead neighbourhood' 'A footfall in the quiet air is crisper than home-made bread' 'and the budgerigar bats an eyelid . . . then balances in sleep' It is silence keeps the old couple awake'	'Silence between them like a thread to hold'
Growing old:	'The old couple in the brand-new bungalow' 'Fumble their way to bed' 'they nag each other' 'Their chesty breathing'	'time itself's a feather Touching them gently'
The end of physical passion:	'divorced in sleep by twin-beds'	'Lying apart now, each in a separate bed' 'They hardly ever touch' 'Chastity faces them' 'my father and my mother Whose fire from which I came has now grown cold'

7. The poet is not related to the couple in *The Old Couple*; the poet is the child of the couple in *One Flesh*.

Acknowledgements

The authors and publishers are grateful to the authors, publishers and others who have given permission for the use of copyright material identified in the text. It has not been possible to identify the sources of all the material used and in such cases the publishers would welcome information from copyright owners.

John Milne for 'Solomon Grundy' by Martin Bell on p. 6; Michael Swan for 'Days' on pp. 8–10; Alan Duff for 'Sunday, Bloody Sunday' on pp. 13–14; Penguin Books Ltd for the extracts on pp. 16, 19 and 20 from *Conversations with Children* (Penguin Books 1978) pp. 1, 16, 71, 74, 78, copyright © R. D. Laing, 1978, and for the extract on p. 26 from *Flight into Camden* (Longman Books, 1960), copyright © David Storey, 1960; Vernon Scannell for 'Growing Pain' on p. 18; University of Georgia Press for 'A Child Half-Asleep' on p. 20 from *New and Selected Poems* by Tony Connor, copyright © The University of Georgia Press, 1982; David Higham Associates Ltd for 'It was Long Ago' on pp. 22–23 by Eleanor Farjeon, from *Silver Sand and Snow* published by Michael Joseph Ltd, and for 'What Has Happened to Lulu?' on p. 27 by Charles Causley, from *Figgie Hobbin* published by Macmillan; ATV Music Ltd and Northern Songs Ltd for 'She's Leaving Home' on pp. 27–28, 'I'm Looking Through You' on p. 44, 'I'm Only Sleeping' on p. 101, 'Eleanor Rigby' on p. 111, 'When I'm Sixty-Four' on p. 133 by John Lennon/Paul McCartney; Granada Publishing Ltd for 'Sorry' on p. 31 by R. S. Thomas from *The Bread of Truth*; George Allen & Unwin for 'Goodbye' on p. 34 from *Ha! Ha! Among the Trumpets* by Alun Lewis; Anne Ridler for 'At Parting' on pp. 35–36; Laurence Pollinger Ltd and the Estate of H. E. Bates for the extract on pp. 40–42 from *Love for Lydia* published by Michael Joseph Ltd; Laurence Pollinger Ltd for the extract on pp. 42–43 from *The Heart of the Matter* by Graham Greene, published by William Heinemann Ltd and The Bodley Head Ltd; Barry Cole for 'Reported Missing' on pp. 44–45; Hugo Williams for 'Present Continuous' on p. 48; The Hogarth Press for the extract from *Cider with Rosie* on p. 50 by Laurie Lee; David Harsent for 'The Rag Doll to the Heedless Child' on p. 51; Faber and Faber Ltd for 'Boy at the Window' on p. 53 from *Poems 1943–1956* by Richard Wilbur, recorded by permission of Harcourt Brace Jovanovich, Inc. from *Things of this World*, copyright © 1952, 1980 by Richard Wilbur; André Deutsch for 'Tonight at Noon' on pp. 58–59 by Adrian Henri; H. Nicholson and Autolycus Publications for 'Daydream' on p. 60 by A. S. J. Tessimond from *Not Love Perhaps ...*; Faber and Faber Ltd for 'Scaffolding' on p. 65 from *Death of a Naturalist* by Seamus Heaney; Mollie Waters Literary Agent for the extract on p. 70 from *The Birds* by Daphne du Maurier; Jonathan Schell and Jonathan Cape Ltd for the extract on p. 70 from *The Fate of the Earth*; Olwyn Hughes Literary Agency for 'Mushrooms' on pp. 71–72 from *The Colossus and Other Poems* by Sylvia Plath, published by Faber and Faber London, copyright © Ted Hughes, 1967; Sixth Daily Mirror Children's Literary Competition for 'And the Flies will be Supreme' on p. 72 from *Children as Writers*; the Hogarth Press for 'Beleaguered Cities' on p. 75 from *Time and Memory* by F. L. Lucas; Little, Brown and Company in association with the Atlantic Monthly Press for 'Water Picture' on pp. 79–80 from *New and Selected Things Taking Place*,

Acknowledgements

copyright © 1956 by May Swenson, first appeared in *The New Yorker*; Alistair Reid for 'The Waterglass' on pp. 82–83; Faber and Faber Ltd for 'Reflections' on p. 87 from *The Collected Poems of Louis MacNeice*, recorded by permission of David Higham Associates Ltd; Harper & Row, Publishers, Inc. for 'Commuter' on p. 88 from *Poems and Sketches of E. B. White*, originally appeared in *The New Yorker*, copyright © 1925, 1953 by E. B. White; Patrick Early for 'The Commuters' on pp. 91–92; *The New Yorker* for 'Fatigue' on p. 93 by Peggy Bacon, copyright © 1932, 1960 The New Yorker Magazine, Inc.; Andrew Wright for the extract from *John Cecil* on pp. 96–97; Gerald Duckworth & Co. Ltd for 'Living' on pp. 102–103 from *Monro Collected Poems* by Harold Monro; University of Nebraska Press for 'January' on p. 107 from *The Collected Poems of Weldon Kees*; *The New Yorker* for 'A Sad Song About Greenwich Village' on pp. 110–111 by Frances Park, copyright © 1927, 1955 The New Yorker Magazine, Inc.; Collins Publishers for the extract on p. 116 from *The Problem of Pain* by C. S. Lewis; Penguin Books Ltd for the extract on pp. 117–118 from *The Challenge of Pain* (Penguin Education, Revised Edition 1982) pp. 56–57, copyright © Ronald Melzack and Patrick D. Wall, 1982; Francis King for 'Patient' on pp. 118–119; David Higham Associates Ltd for 'Pain' on p. 119 and 'One Flesh' on p. 128 from *Collected Poems* by Elizabeth Jennings published by Macmillan; The Hogarth Press for 'Visiting Hour' on pp. 122–123 by Norman MacCaig from *Rings on a Tree*; Penguin Books Ltd for the extracts on pp. 125–126 from *The View in Winter* by Ronald Blythe (Penguin Books 1981) pp. 215, 216, 313–314, copyright © Ronald Blythe, 1979; F. Pratt Green for 'The Old Couple' on p. 127.

Photographs and illustrations: Arthur Christiansen p. 4; Sue Adler and *The Observer* p. 15; Nigel Luckhurst pp. 24, 49, 63, 85, 95; BBC Hulton Picture Library p. 32; Andre Kertesz p. 52; Private Collection, USA for 'The Mystery and Melancholy of a Street' by Giorgio de Chirico, on p. 57; Pan Books Ltd and Roger Phillips for p. 69 from *Mushrooms* by Roger Phillips; The Ross Institute of Tropical Hygiene p. 74; Edward Bowness p. 76; Douglas Dickins pp. 77, 90 (top), 154; Barnaby's Picture Library pp. 78 and 154; Camerapix Hutchison Library p. 88; Richard Foxcroft p. 89 (top); J. Allan Cash Ltd p. 89 (bottom); Taeke Henstra/Panorama Camera Press, London p. 90 (bottom); Tate Gallery for 'The Resurrection, Cookham' by Stanley Spencer, on pp. 98–9; Andrzej Dudzinski and *The Sunday Times Magazine* p. 108; Paul Carter and the Blackfriars Photography Project p. 109; F.lli Alinari (Firenze) p. 115; Stad Brugge, Groeningemuseum for 'Life's Sunset' by Edmond Van Hove, 1905, on p. 124. Cartoon on p. 40 by Bill Belcher.

Actors on the recording: Adrienne Burgess, John Graham, John Newton, Nicolette Mackenzie, Anne Rosenfeld.

Book design by Peter Ducker MSTD